MARRIED
BY
FORCE

MARRIED
BY
FORCE

LEILA

With the collaboration of Marie-Thérèse Cuny

Translated by Sue Rose

PORTRAIT

Visit the Portrait website!

· ·

PORTRAIT Piatkus publishes a wide range of non-fiction, including biography, history, science, music, popular culture and sport.

If you want to:
- read descriptions of our popular titles
- buy our books over the internet
- take advantage of our special offers
- enter our monthly competition
- learn more about your favourite Piatkus authors

VISIT OUR WEBSITE AT: www.portraitbooks.com

For Ryad, my son, my secret garden

Contents

Acknowledgements

I THANK MARTINE FROM the bottom of my heart for supporting me, listening to me and cuddling me. Thank you also on behalf of my son and my family. I'm your 'second daughter'; you're the 'big sister' I never had. I shall always be close to you. Because of you, my relationship with my parents has changed. I see them now as I've never seen them before.

My thanks to Sophie for her support and for our conversations. Because of you I've been able to close a door and have a future. Thank you for being my friend.

Jean-Marie: 'Blimey!', you're one of the few people who can make me laugh, even when I'm feeling low.

My thanks to Marcelle for protecting me, for being there and for loving me. Thanks for supporting me during the worst times of my life.

Marie-Louise, Sébastien, Anne, Marie-Delphine and Sophie, thank you for believing in me and for giving me the chance to pull through.

My thanks to Isabelle and Thomas for their friendship.

My thanks to Dominique: because of you, I've been able

to have this incredible adventure. Thanks for your friendship and your support.

My thanks to Marie-Thérèse Cuny, my 'granny', who has listened to me and transcribed my life so elegantly.

My thanks to everyone in the team at OH! Éditions:

Philippe Robinet for accompanying me on this adventure and for giving me the chance for this once-in-a-lifetime experience. Thank you so much for your honesty and your friendship.

Juliette Legros, my sweet, gentle Juliette. You can stay: that's my final decision!

Jean-Marie Périer, you've amazed me. I'm very proud that I've had the honour of meeting you. I'm deeply touched that a great man like you has taken an interest in my life with such kindness and tact.

Bruno Barbette for understanding my fears and for giving me time.

Edith Leblond for seeing me and 'capturing' me so accurately.

Béatrice Calderon for enabling this book to reach the widest possible readership.

Bernard, Florent, Catherine, Caroline . . . thanks to you and everyone in your team whom I don't yet know: I know how much you have all supported me.

Prologue

THERE'S A FLIGHT OF steps leading up, an entrance hall and a sign saying 'Bureau du Maire'.

My name is Leila and I'm 21. I was born in France and I'm Moroccan by tradition, a tradition that continues to exert a controlling influence over my life through my father. He's not a religious fanatic or a bad man. He's respectable and well respected, like all the fathers in our neighbourhood. He beats his daughter when she disobeys him and this is how he raised me. He trained me to be obedient and submissive and he beat me to make me marry the man walking up the steps before me.

I'm marrying a man I barely know in a French registry office. It's not really a marriage; it's a formality I'm going through under duress. I could run away, race back down the steps screaming for help, but if I did that, my life wouldn't be any more my own than it is now. A daughter brought up in the Muslim tradition cannot live outside the family and the protection of her father, whose role is to find another protector for his daughter: the husband he's chosen for her.

I was born in this neighbourhood and my birth was

registered at this town hall. People assume I have rights, but what use are they? Who can I turn to? A social worker? This is a personal matter: her hands would be tied. The police? They'd tell me that I'm an adult and that I should just say 'no'. Theoretically, there's no such thing as a forced marriage in a democracy. But if I said 'no' before the Mayor, I still wouldn't be free, because I had already been officially married in Morocco and even though that marriage isn't recognised in France, I'd be permanently condemned by my father and the whole neighbourhood community. They'd label me a 'bad girl' and cast me out if I refused to comply with the final formality in France. I could never go back to Morocco of my own accord; my 'husband' would have the right to track me down and repudiate me. There's no greater humiliation for a traditionalist father than having his daughter repudiated.

I'd dreamed of marrying for love, of meeting Mr Right. I would have had a beautiful white dress and a bouquet of flowers they way they do in love stories. I would have stood smiling at the top of the steps and all my friends would have kissed me and congratulated me. I'd have left my family for a tiny flat, just big enough for the two of us; I'd have wept with emotion, kissed my father, mother and all my brothers, and rushed towards the life of happiness and freedom that has always been my dream.

The formality only took ten minutes.

The stranger now has what he wanted, which didn't have to be me, Leila. Any French-born Moroccan woman would have done, so long as she was a virgin and came from a good family. My father didn't even 'sell' me to this man, which sometimes happens. He simply believes in the tradition of arranged marriages between families. He's sincere in his determination to ensure that I'm obedient, that I toe the line. He wouldn't stand for any other type of behaviour from his daughter.

My mind is a blank. I'm not here. This day isn't happening: I've wiped it from my memory in advance. I buried my head in the sand like an ostrich, hoping for fate to step in and somehow rescue me: the end of the world, an earthquake, someone jumping up to declare: 'Forced marriages are against French law!'

We were the only people in that room, apart from two witnesses brought in specially, and there wasn't an earthquake. The Mayor didn't ask any questions. He'd seen other hasty marriages like this with no one uttering cries of joy. I said 'yes' in a voice that didn't sound like mine and signed a piece of paper that I couldn't see for the tears blurring my eyes under my father's stern gaze. At the slightest sign of rebellion, he would have beaten me black and blue and sent me back to Morocco or thrown me out. I ought to have escaped to a hostel and taken advantage of a freedom that I'd never been taught and that scares me half to death. Integration means being free to say 'no'. Tradition makes it impossible to say 'no'. I've never been free to break that unwritten law.

CHAPTER ONE

Where were you?

I WAS ABOUT SEVEN or eight, perhaps younger. I was already used to hearing my father or mother shouting at me from somewhere in the flat. 'Leila! Lay the table! Leila! Watch your brother! Leila! Do the washing-up! Leila! Stay here! Leila! What are you doing?'

Come here. Don't go out. Tidy your room. What time will you be back from school? Clear your things away. Help your mother. Don't talk to that girl. Who were you with?

My head bristled like a pincushion with orders and embargoes. My life wasn't my own. I belonged to the family; I was their tool and they controlled my every move.

When I looked in the mirror I didn't see anyone. I'd been born, I had a body and a head with eyes to see and a heart to feel, and I couldn't use them. I was being brought up in accordance with Moroccan tradition in the heartland of France, and the only place I could breathe freely was at school. In class I had a life. I was a person in my own right. My intelligence revelled in being useful. At break, I was allowed to run around and laugh like the others. I loved school but, as soon as I walked out of the school gates and was on my way back home, I had already ceased to exist.

'Don't dawdle and don't be late home! Look after your brothers!'

I'm the only daughter in a tribe of boys. Every time my mother fell pregnant, I stood in the corridor of the clinic hoping with all my heart, waiting for deliverance, for a voice to say, 'It's a girl!'

But the ritual was always the same: two older brothers, then another brother and another, until there were ten of them. By the time my little sister Sirinne finally arrived, I was 16.

At the age of five or six, I began howling with real despair at never seeing my mother cradling someone who looked like me. I spent my whole childhood and adolescence hoping for a sister, a gift from heaven. It felt as if this endless procession of boys from my mother's womb was a punishment inflicted on me, and that being born among them was an even greater punishment.

Ali and Brahim, Karim and Miloud, Mohammad and Hassan, Mansour and Slimane, Idriss and Rachid. My mother had a baby virtually every year, so the characters playing such an important role in my life scrolled past, one after the other, like the credits of a film, while I remained all alone behind the scenes, invisible yet burdened with all the household chores. I was jealous of my school friends at the end of the day: their mothers came to collect them, hugging and kissing them at the school gates. They appeared to mean a great deal to their parents. My mother was doing production-line work with her tribe of children. There was always a baby crying, even at night. Her life was sheer slavery.

As a result, from a very young age I was supposed to help round the house, but I flatly refused to be a slave to my ten brothers. My mother would smack me and pull my hair, but I did almost nothing she wanted. As far as she was concerned, it was perfectly natural to expect some help from her only daughter: that was how she'd been brought up in her village before she arrived in France, where she knew no one and couldn't speak the language. When I was born, in the early 1980s, there were very few North African families in our neighbourhood, but when she'd first arrived here from her village, there wasn't even one. As my mother kept having children, she ended up trapped in a four-bedroom flat barely large enough for eleven children, in a country where the sun never shone, unable to venture outside to go shopping by herself. My father took care of everything outside the home. He spent all he earned as a factory worker on provisions, which he went out to buy himself. There was no question of birth control. No one had ever heard of the 'pill'. God sent him sons. I wondered later if the fact that my father had lost his father so early might have had something to do with this relentless procreation.

When my mother first began living in France, she watched life pass by through the third-floor window. She only left home to give birth or to follow in my father's wake, trailing her clan of boys behind her. I was as cut off as she was. As the boys grew older, they were allowed to run around outside unchaperoned, but I wasn't. If any of the girls who lived locally came by to see if I wanted to play outside the block of flats and said, 'We're going down to play elastic skipping. Are you coming?', I'd reply, 'I'll have to ask Papa, but he won't let me. Go and ask him for me. He may say "yes" to you, but he'll say "no" if I ask him.'

And the answer was always the same: 'If you want some fresh air, go out on the balcony!'

It wasn't fair. I didn't dare ask him why and I didn't try to understand. No was no. I can still see myself standing on that balcony forced to watch the other girls playing, kept prisoner by some unknown law. I was just a little girl, still in primary school, and I didn't understand. How dangerous could it be to go downstairs for some fresh air?

Slowly other families moved into the neighbourhood from the Maghreb, then from all over Africa. At school, we mixed with the French-born girls and there were no conflicts. My best friend Souria played elastic skipping with the others; Farida, Joséphine, Sylvie, Malika, Alia and Charlotte played in the street without me. Why?

My father raised all his children to be terrified of him. If we made the big mistake of meeting his eyes when he was questioning one of us, we'd be slapped in the face first before being told, 'Lower your eyes.'

There were never any words of affection, and even less reassuring gestures. I don't remember jumping onto my father's lap once or being kissed hello or goodnight by him. His brutal control was a far cry from what I saw or heard from other children, whether they were French or of foreign extraction. When I was very little, his style of upbringing maddened me. I remember a residential winter sports trip organised in the last year of primary school. I wasn't allowed to go from the start. The teacher came to see my father and kindly told him, 'Your daughter will be quite safe. The girls are kept completely separate from the boys.'

But he refused. My father was worried that, despite segregation, some socialising might go on between the girls and boys when he wasn't there to keep an eye on me. At the age of ten, though, children are pretty innocent. I couldn't see anything wrong with mixing with boys.

At home, I slept in the same bedroom as a tribe of brothers and that didn't bother my father. It did me. He had absolutely no idea that I was at risk in his own home.

He didn't know that at an age when I should have been playing with Barbie dolls, I had been put off sexual promiscuity for life by one of my brothers, who was much older than me. I was terrified at the thought of being trapped in a room with that young man. My abuser, who was getting off scot-free, knew very well that I'd keep my mouth shut through shame and that I'd never dare to accuse him. He was right. He had of course respected my virginity. In a Muslim family, a girl's virginity is sacred. But there are other ways that are just as terrible to humiliate a little girl of that age. I held my tongue like all abused children. I still hold my tongue, but there's no escaping from that poison. Why didn't I shout for help? Why did I put up with it? Why should I feel guilty all the time when my abuser is living his life without an ounce of remorse? He simply made me the butt of his sexuality; I was just a handy object. Nothing more.

I was being punished for some mysterious sin. I was worthless, cowardly, defiled, fit for the rubbish heap. So I did my best to bury the wretched business somewhere deep in my head. I blocked it out. That was my only means of escape.

I became aggressive, rebellious and emotionally unstable. I was driven crazy by the imposed silence, by this prison in which only the head of the family had the right to speak and boys were always right. It was as a result of this that I vowed to myself that I'd do well at school and have a career. I'd only marry one day if I decided that it was what I wanted, but I'd do it as late as possible and, most importantly, I wouldn't breed a tribe of children. This meant meeting a man I really liked, someone I wouldn't be tempted to make suffer for my childhood.

While waiting, I dreamed on my balcony like an abandoned, solitary princess about some Prince Charming from a TV soap. I clowned about with my school friends, telling them about the thrashings, the slaps and the times I'd had the shit knocked out of me in punishment for my brazen rebellion.

I just wanted to live my life, to receive a little attention and affection. I wasn't asking for much. I couldn't have cared less about pretty clothes or dolls. I wanted to be loved, to be kissed good morning and goodnight, to be collected from school and, as none of that happened, I kept wondering if I was really my father's daughter. It seemed to me that I was the only one he treated with such indifference. Despite the authority that he also exercised over my brothers, they continually ganged up on me. I was never right – and my mother agreed. She always made a fuss if I wanted to go out with my friends, to go into town or to one of their homes, to listen to music and indulge in a little girlish chatter. 'Leila, you can't go out on Wednesday afternoon! You have to learn how to make bread and to cook; you don't realise it, but when you get married, you won't spend more than a night with your husband. You'll be back here the next day because your husband will repudiate you.'

These threats meant nothing to me and seemed to belong to another age. So, on Wednesday afternoons, I took malicious pleasure in infuriating my mother. 'So you don't want me to go out? Don't worry, I won't go out.'

I'd flop down in front of the television. As a result, before leaving for work my father would threaten me. 'I'm warning you, if your mother tells me tonight that you haven't done as you're told, you'll be in big trouble.'

'Sure, whatever!'

'I'm talking to you, Leila! Look at me when I'm talking to you, not the TV!'

'Make up your mind! When I look at you, you tell me to lower my eyes, and if I don't look at you, you tell me to look at you. Which is it?'

'I'm warning you, you'll get a good hiding before I leave.'

'Whatever, Papa, that's fine by me, OK, no problem!'

I was thinking to myself: 'Yeah, yeah, yeah!'

'Leila, it's time to serve dinner!'

Having to serve meals to my brothers while they watched television in peace particularly infuriated me. Service was free of charge for them. They sat down to eat, and then got up again without lifting a finger. It was also my job to clear the table. Once I'd finished that chore, I'd get dressed to go out, and my mother would stand between the door and me.

'Aren't you going to do the washing-up?'

'No.'

'Leila! I swear your father will murder you.'

'Yeah, yeah, yeah.'

I'd leave under a barrage of insults, slamming the door behind me. I knew when I slammed the door that I'd get a good hiding from my father later that evening. My mother would slap me or pull my hair, nothing too serious, and I'd laugh it off, but with my father it was a different matter altogether. Various expressions diplomatically described what went on. Being beaten black and blue, or getting a good hiding from your father or having the shit knocked out of you meant winding up with a bruised and swollen face, not to mention the rest.

On one occasion my father actually tied my feet and hands together, because I'd been smoking a cigarette when I came out of school. I was battered black and blue. He knocked the living daylights out of me because of that fag – really heavy blows that left marks and were extremely painful. He even broke my arm once. It never worried anybody, although my French teacher once tried to throw me a lifeline.

'If something's wrong, Leila, you know you can talk to me about it.'

I'd gazed at him haughtily. 'I'm absolutely fine. I fell over in basketball and wrenched my forearm.'

I would have been ashamed to describe my life, even though I didn't deserve to be beaten like that.

When my parents had to go out, I stayed slumped in front of the TV, which was usually reserved for my father, who'd channel-hop in line with 'his' rules: no love stories, no kissing on screen, nothing that might put ideas into a teenage girl's head.

The television was my way out, the dream missing from my life. I was no longer Leila, 15 or 16 at that time and a prisoner on the third floor, but a soap-opera heroine. My father couldn't stand this type of escapism on the rare occasions I was left alone in the house.

My mother: 'Leila, I'm leaving the dish on the heat. Keep an eye on it; we'll have lunch when we come back!'

My father: 'I'm warning you, if anything happens to that dish, you're in for it!'

'OK!'

My mother: 'Leila, you can't go out on Wednesday afternoon!'

My father would keep on and on. 'If I ever hear anyone gossiping about you . . . I'm warning you.'

I knew all those little chats by heart. 'I'm warning you . . . If I ever . . . Where were you?'

I heard that 'where were you?' millions of times. I was forbidden to go out, and forbidden to play ball and to skip between the ages of 8 and 12. I thought it was ridiculously unfair having to stay on that wretched balcony, but I still didn't realise I was being held prisoner. When I was a teenager, they stopped talking about forbidding me to do things and started calling it 'protection'. Leila is a rebel; we have to protect her because she's so headstrong. However, the more 'protected' I was, the more I rebelled, either silently or in hysterics.

It was like talking to a brick wall. My mother might give me orders, my father might repeat them, but I just said 'yeah, yeah, yeah' to shut them up and did what I wanted anyway. The way they saw it, I was abnormal because I wouldn't obey the rules laid down for girls of my 'sort'. My sort meant being a French national, born in France, raised in the French cultural tradition at school and in the North African cultural tradition at home, which was tantamount to having no freedom and no individuality, and being in service to the family.

'What will people say if they see you going out too often? You'll get a bad reputation!'

A bad reputation . . .

Although when I was born there weren't many North Africans in the neighbourhood, by the time I was a teenager they were everywhere, and families, children and rules that had to be obeyed and applied to the whole community, surrounded us. Like everyone else, my parents had to inculcate me with the common laws, but we never had a chat to explain them – it was just brutal authority, the type that leads to conflict.

I shone at school. I was one of the top students in the class. In secondary school I came within a hair's breadth of disaster, because the older I grew, the more oppressive the rules seemed.

I had to be at home all the time, at the beck and call of my parents and brothers. I had to do the housework and the cooking, and change the babies' nappies. I was a mother before I ever had a child of my own. I was supposed to grow up and obey blindly at the same time. But I couldn't build a life like this, so I took a wrecking ball to it. I resented the whole world for being the household's *only* daughter.

I had to do the housework in the morning, while my brothers were still asleep. I cursed them, watching them sleep soundly while I washed the floor. I was even rough with them. Instead of quietly saying, 'Get up, I'm washing the floor', I'd yell, 'Get up! Do you think I've got nothing better to do? I'm not your maid.'

To be honest, though, they were incredibly rude when asking me to do something. 'Iron this! I'm going out and I need to wear it!'

All it would have taken was a 'Please, Leila,' or 'Do me a favour . . . ' and I would have done it for them willingly. But there was never a 'please' and they were even less likely to say 'thank you'. I could've put up with one brother or two or even four, but when they all turned up wanting their shirts, trousers and shoes cleaned . . .

As a teenager, I already had eight brothers aged between 6 and 20 breathing down my neck. It was an array of young males: little boys who had to be dressed, teenagers who chucked their trainers and socks across the bedroom, and grown men who yelled for their shirts and jeans. Those layabouts treated me as a slave. If I told them where to get off, I'd get a slap from one or other of them.

At first they could do anything they wanted to me, and I didn't react. Then I began to lose my temper. I was prepared to get a good hiding, but I wasn't going to let my adversary escape unscathed. By the time I'd turned 13, I was giving as good as I got. They went running to my father, but I was the only one put on trial.

'She hit me! She's older than me. If she hits me now, what might she do to me later?'

'I didn't hit him. He started it. I was just defending myself.'

Obviously, no one questions the word of a son. I was always the one to blame. However, because I would receive a thrashing even if I just pushed them away, there was nothing to stop me. Even if I didn't win against Miloud or one of the others, at least I'd belted him. I'd now devised my personal strategy for combating slavery. In the morning, I was supposed to make breakfast for the others even before I had mine. I'd get up at the last minute, with just enough time to wash, dress and race off to school, shouting triumphantly, 'I don't have time for breakfast!'

They were left stranded in the middle of the kitchen fuming about me: it was sheer bliss. Once I was out of the door, I could breathe again: back to real life at last.

In fact, school was the only place where I could relax. Even there, though, I'd become aggressive to everyone. I fought with the other kids; I refused to listen to what the teacher told me. I felt picked on and rejected all the time, and at odds with myself.

I did my best to survive, which wasn't very well. Later on, because it was taboo like everything else, I began to smoke the odd cigarette despite the beatings, and I learned to avoid being found out. My father or one of my brothers insisted on smelling my breath before I'd pass the 'fag test', so I copied my friends: I armed myself with mints as a precaution and became very crafty. Before asking for a packet of fags at the tobacconists, I'd quickly check out the shop to make sure I couldn't see any of my father's friends, or mates of my brothers or cousins, or friends of the friends. At the slightest sign of danger, I'd ask for a three-franc stamp and, in the end, I perfected my technique with the help of the shop assistant. I didn't have enough money to collect stamps I was never going to use, so when I asked for a stamp, she knew the drill. She'd put a packet of fags to one side for me until I came back and handed over the stamp in exchange.

The other North African girls were like me. They learned to be clever, to tell lies and to keep quiet. They used trickery to meet up after school, lied about lesson times and learned to spot the brother acting as a snoop or 'hidden camera', so that he could gleefully denounce his big sister's minor indiscretions. Up to a certain age, these were minor – girls' talk for quarter of an hour, chattering about trivial subjects. I wasn't a flirt or a risk-taker. Later on, between the ages of 16 and 18, some of the girls would secretly apply make-up in the hallway of the flats or wear some forbidden article of clothing. I wasn't one of them, because I couldn't see the point of making my life even more complicated. I was sensible. I ignored boys; I avoided them like the plague, convinced that I had to protect my reputation and my virginity. At an age when I should have been having my first romances, I wasn't on the same wavelength as the girls who were allowed to do what they wanted without upsetting their parents. Going out with a boy at the age of 16, holding hands and exchanging a few kisses wasn't for me.

At that time I had some African friends whose lives were

even tougher than mine. I know some of them put up with incest for years and didn't talk about it. We didn't ask each other difficult questions; we lived our own lives in silence. We had to laugh, tell jokes and make fun of everything and of ourselves. That was survival.

Over the years, being caged by my family had turned me into a girl who was nothing like the real me. Rebellious because I'd been forced to be submissive, I thrashed around like a fly imprisoned in a glass jar. I could see life and freedom through the glass, but I was continually crashing into the transparent sides.

I wrote my personal diary in my head, in silence. If I'd actually written it down on paper, it would have been stolen. As a result, by asking myself questions and answering them on my own without ever finding the right answers, I almost went crazy and came within a hair's breadth of killing myself. I was a tightrope walker petrified by vertigo; I was walking a thin wire above a vast, empty space. Moroccan Leila on one side and French Leila on the other; a girl kept prisoner by her family on one side and a runaway on the other.

I had two faces, two personalities – one who didn't say a word about her suffering, the other who screamed about it. At the age of 13, I 'tried' suicide. I locked myself in the bathroom pretending I was taking a bath. I really wanted to die. I said to myself that I couldn't end up anywhere worse than here on earth. I believed in God and thought I would land up in paradise because, even though suicide was a sin, He would forgive me. This happened after I'd run away for the first time and been so badly beaten when I came back that life no longer seemed worth living.

The member of staff in charge of school discipline had

taken me into her office and slapped me eight times in quick succession. Bleeding but rebellious, I'd protested, 'You've got no right to hit me. I'm going to tell my father.'

'I'm warning you in advance that this is just a taster; you can expect much worse at home. Surprising though it may seem, your father personally authorised me to give you a good hiding!'

No one had made any attempt to find out why I'd bunked off. I wouldn't have been able to put it clearly into words anyway. With hindsight, I wanted to upset my father and worry him. He didn't protect me; he wasn't interested in me; it was my way of getting his attention, of demanding his love. Doing a bunk was a way of scaring him. I'd cleared off with my friends, a small multicultural band of about ten French, Moroccan, Algerian, Tunisian and African boys and girls on a jaunt, playing truant in the countryside – a well-organised gang on a four-day spring holiday. We all pretended to leave for school and come home. Our parents didn't suspect a thing, and we got the hell out of our neighbourhood with its familiar blocks of flats and scarpered into the nearby countryside. We jumped fully dressed into the river, and then rolled around in the grass screaming with laughter. I was on another planet, released from captivity. When we were soaked from head to foot, the girls went back to the house of one of our gang members, a French girl who could lend us a change of clothes. Jeans and sweaters all look the same. Parents only notice what girls are wearing if their skirts are too short or their T-shirts are too tight: everything else is interchangeable. The boys sorted themselves out. During those four crazy days filled with laughter, we even took a trip to Paris. We all pretended to be going on a compulsory museum visit that had been entered in advance in our home–school contact books. My parents had signed what I'd written myself: 'Compulsory visit to the Louvre on . . . Contribution 50 francs.'

'Fifty francs! That's expensive,' my father had said.

'Yeah, but that's just the way it is. It's marked "compulsory", as you can see.'

With our 50 francs we made our getaway to Paris like great adventurers, and once we had arrived at the Gare de Lyon . . . we stayed there. No one knew what to do or where to go, because we had to be back home by 5 p.m. for the end of school. So it was better to stay there, calling each other tramps and laughing like crazy. We spent the whole day in a station. Some adventurers! Anyway, we didn't have any great expectations – we were just playing at being grown up, just bunking off, taking a break from home, from the neighbourhood, from school, from the floors of flats where everyone knew everyone else and no one minded their own business.

We spent the 50 francs, of course. We had to eat and then had nothing left to pay for the return train journey. We all prayed we wouldn't come across a ticket inspector – a fine would have given the game away to our parents and would have meant a thrashing into the bargain.

The last day was spent infiltrating the nearby secondary school, still playing at being grown up. Primary school was for kids. The plan was to enter the school, mingle with the students, chat with them pretending to be in this or that class, hang out in the cafeteria and keep it up as long as possible. The school gates were closed, but anyone could walk in and no one asked us who we were.

The gang had bunked off from Tuesday to Friday and we had to go back to school on Monday, or at least the others did, but I didn't. I gave myself an additional morning of complete solitude. I needed it because I was never alone in my everyday life. That quiet morning spent thinking things over on my own was essential because I knew what I had coming.

For those four days I'd left the phone off the hook when I set off in the morning and had replaced the receiver just before my father came home. Since no one had been able to contact my parents by phone, a letter was bound to arrive in the morning. I gazed at the river, the grass and the dew, and savoured every minute of those last few stolen hours of freedom, which were going to cost me dearly.

In the afternoon I faced the music. Although I'd wanted to appear laid-back when I arrived at the school gates, I didn't have time. After being dragged by the hair into the office and slapped with a vengeance, my ear bloodied with my father's permission, I received the rest at home, as promised. My father slapped me, kicked me, scratched me and hit me with everything he could lay his hands on. He was beating a body that felt numb: he could've broken every bone in my body. I wouldn't have cared less as long as he didn't rip out my brain. Neither he nor my mother could understand my terrible moodiness, the silence that was driving me mad. Everything was always my fault. I wanted him to love me, ask me questions, attempt to find out what was upsetting me and then comfort me.

All he did was hit me, so I locked myself in the bathroom to swallow what I'd found in the medicine cabinet. I went out like a light and the next day, still alive, I staggered to school, virtually comatose. Eventually I collapsed in class and they had to call an ambulance. I ended up in a hospital bed, seething with rage; I hated the whole world, my father and God.

Instead of my father, who wasn't there, and a God who didn't reply, they sent me a shrink, who said, 'Let's have a little chat, Leila.'

Total mental block. I felt even more alone. I didn't need a shrink. I needed my father; I wanted him to be standing there in front of me, asking, 'What's going on? Why? Are you unhappy? Tell me what's upsetting you. Tell me everything, I'll protect you, you're my daughter, I love you.' It was his voice I wanted to hear, not the professional, resolutely sympathetic tones of a specialist head doctor, saying, 'They won't allow you to go home until you talk to me. I'm here to listen.'

On the first day I clenched my teeth, but on the second day, as I didn't want to stay in there, I cooked up some story claiming that I'd been feeling a bit low, that it was over and that I now felt fine. My father didn't come to visit me.

The shrink swallowed the lie. He told my parents that I was simply going through a teenage crisis. I was confined to bed for three days, my mind in a turmoil, resenting everyone, including myself, not knowing how to die so that I could be free. I had realised that I could never talk about my deep feelings of guilt, my belief that I'd be kept prisoner for ever. Anyway, if anyone tried to understand, I lied. I preferred to clown around with my friends. I was an expert at transforming a humiliating family punch-up into an amusing piece of alternative theatre. I had a talent for that type of entertainment. Even now, I occasionally act like a sad clown determined to make my audience laugh so that my despair doesn't get the better of me. I carefully kept everything else bottled up.

The day I had my first period was really weird, since neither my mother nor any other woman had ever spoken to me about 'that'. As a result I woke up one morning and completely freaked out about this catastrophe. 'They'll kill me, they'll kill me. Maman will think someone's touched me down there!'

Could my virginity have vanished just like that, without warning?

My mother was grumbling outside the bathroom door. 'You're taking your time! Come out of there!'

I stammered, 'Um, er . . . '

'Open the door.'

'No, I can't, I can't.'

None of us girls ever talked about periods at school. If I'd had an older sister she probably would have told me about them, but I was completely panic-stricken. My mother finally opened the door using a small spoon, and then burst out laughing, which didn't make me feel any better.

'It's nothing to worry about. I'll give you everything you need . . . but from now on, my girl, you'd better be careful! You'll have this every month. That's just how it is!'

What else did I have to be careful about? Later on, in a biology lesson, the teacher talked about the human body and I really understood what had happened to me, but at the time the only two things that lodged in my mind were 'every month' and 'be careful'.

Of course, my father had been informed immediately, because this was the accepted drill for a daughter who had to be watched. The conversation was pretty much the same as ever.

'Be careful around the neighbourhood! I'm warning you . . . '

'What? Don't worry, I haven't done anything!'

'I'm warning you: it brings shame on the family if a

daughter isn't a virgin when she marries, so you'd better be careful.'

None of us had a bedroom of our own in the flat. There were three or four of us crammed into each room. It was absolutely essential that the male contingent didn't catch a glimpse of my sanitary towels. Deadly silence. It was the same when it came to buying bras a little later on. I couldn't say, 'Maman, I'm old enough to wear a bra now.' I don't think she even gave it a thought or that she ever wore one.

I was left to cope with my emerging womanhood on my own, when I'd actually become something of a tomboy, more knowledgeable about fighting than about the right underwear for my age.

A white French friend of mine gave me her old bras. I was stuck in the Middle Ages and living in France in the 1990s, unlike other girls of my age whose socially and culturally different parents didn't apply the same rules. I was searching in vain for an identity.

I gradually learned about my parents' origins on our customary holidays to the North African interior, but instead of clarifying the issue of my own identity, these visits only complicated matters further. When I was young I was sometimes asked whether I was a Berber or an Arab.

My mother is an Arab, my father a Berber and I'm French. Which should I choose? I feel more like an Arab than a Berber for the simple reason that my father only taught us to speak Arabic. However, I'm more comfortable speaking French than Arabic, for one good reason: I was born here and I learned it at school. I would, however, also like to feel that I am a Berber, because although the women are submissive, they are allowed more freedom of behaviour. They dance with the men at parties and weddings, don't have to wear headscarves and are more highly respected within their community.

My mother went to school until she was eight or nine. Then her own mother decided to keep her at home because she was becoming too pretty to be allowed to run free in their mountain village. She had to learn how to be a housewife, and was no longer allowed to go out, even to family parties. She was forbidden to talk to anyone, and couldn't even fetch water from the well. Men were already asking to marry her, at the age of eight or nine. When she told me this, I couldn't even imagine how such a thing was possible. She didn't dream of any life outside the four walls of her home.

She often says, 'I'm very grateful to my mother. If she hadn't been so strict, I wouldn't have been such a good wife.'

I felt incapable of sticking to that way of life.

For many years I only knew my mother's village: a few houses nestling among the olive trees in beautiful surroundings, but with no running water or electricity. Even now, life is very hard there. My mother would spend her days grinding grain, pressing olives, preparing meals and doing the housework on all fours – there was no such thing as a broom, so she was forced to use a small brush that was only knee-high. I'd already done it on a few occasions, and every time I was forced to give up on the chore because my back was killing me.

My mother didn't want for anything material; her family was thought to be wealthy. She was well dressed and she owned jewellery, but she was also the household slave, the only daughter in a long line of boys. Her beauty was a talking point in the village and her father regarded her as a precious treasure. She never went out.

My father tried to find out who this mysterious beauty was. He kept watch with the other boys in the trees over-hanging the spring, hoping to catch a glimpse of her when she fetched water, but unfortunately she wasn't even allowed to do that. One day my mother, who was 15 at the time, begged my grandmother to let her attend a wedding celebration.

My grandmother relented with a stream of advice. 'I want you to stay right at the back of the hall, out of the way! I don't want you showing your face! I'm warning you, if anyone tells me that you've been seen near the musicians or any men, if I hear any gossip about you, I swear I'll kill you!'

So she attended the party, shrouded in the haik, the traditional white sheet that was draped over her whole body, showing only her eyes. This was the 1960s and women were still wearing the haik in her village. This is when my father finally caught sight of her, sheathed from head to toe, tucked quietly in a corner. My grandfather made thousands of excuses – his daughter, the apple of his eye, would only be allowed to leave home as late as possible – but her suitor persisted for over a year. After some argument my grandfather finally relented in the face of such determination. The wedding preparations began. My mother kept saying, 'I don't want to be married, I don't know him.' Her father replied, 'You'll marry him nonetheless!' The whole village was up in arms when they discovered that the most beautiful girl there had been handed over to a stranger. They wanted to kill my father, so his future father-in-law had to step in with all the weight of his authority, which fortunately counted for a great deal. He announced frankly to the rebellious local Casanovas, 'It's not up to him. It was my decision! He wanted her; it's his destiny. She's my daughter and I'll give her to anyone I like. If any of you want to come to the wedding, you can, and if you don't, then it's your loss.'

While civil war threatened to break out as a result of this

mismatch in the Arab village, the same battle was being fought on the Berber side. My mother's future mother-in-law went to considerable lengths to have the marriage called off. She even paid a man to make advances to my father's bride-to-be while he was away to put her in a compromising position. Her trap failed.

Once the marriage had been solemnised, the men from the Arab village even sent an emissary to the young wife, her own kid brother, with this message: 'If you leave the Berber to marry "Mr so-and-so", he'll buy you everything you want. He sends you this silver belt.'

Fortunately, the newlyweds had moved to a different village and I suppose she simply learned to love my father, but when I was a teenager, I didn't understand how she could be happy with him.

As for my father, he doesn't talk much about his past. I learned everything I know about his childhood too late to be of any help when I was rebelling against him. No one ever gave him the love that I demanded from him as my due. His own father died when he was only a few months old, and he was neglected by his mother and raised by a woman who made life very difficult for him. His older brother, who was responsible for him, was unfortunately absent much of the time. He bravely buried himself in his studies but when he wanted to revise in the evenings, she'd switch off the light, saying, 'That's expensive! You're not the one paying the electricity bills!' As a result he would study by candlelight. From the little he told us – because he doesn't like to speak about this period of his life – that woman even made him sleep in a box room when his brother, the only person capable of protecting him, wasn't there. He therefore learned the harsh lessons of a loveless childhood, and when he became a father, he in his turn performed his role with a heightened sense of duty. He obtained a work contract through one of his cousins, and sought refuge in France. I think it was hard for him to leave his job as a civil servant. He found himself working in a factory, but earned a better living in France as a factory worker than he had in his native country.

If my parents had told me about their lives earlier, I might have understood their behaviour better, but unfortunately, whether I understood their reasons or not, it wouldn't have altered my future. I was bearing the brunt of two different cultures that both upheld the tradition of subjugating girls. My only experience of their homeland was during the holidays and in the summer sun. I love Morocco. I'm not turning my back on my origins. I'm a believer. I had no intention of chasing after boys – they didn't even interest me – but I wanted it to be *my* business, not theirs. I'd heard many stories of 'arranged marriages', but they definitely had no relevance to me. I didn't live in an isolated mountain village, and didn't feel a vocation to be a servant to men. It seemed perfectly natural to me: it was obvious that my brothers were just as capable of laying the table and putting away their things as I was; just as capable of being useful to the community instead of lounging around and accusing me of terrible wrongdoings when I made the slightest remark. Some of them were gentler than others, less violent and aggressive, but I was crushed by the heavy burden of these young men under my father's protection. He encouraged them to perpetuate this male chauvinism instead of adapting and evolving. Some of my friends were French boys of North African origin and not all of them behaved like this. Not all fathers were necessarily like mine. They didn't systematically beat up their daughters.

Yet despite my rebelliousness, my refusal to obey the so-called rules, I had no other choice but to abide by them or skirt round them like a potential criminal. I wasn't the only one.

My best friend Souria, who was beautiful and happy-go-lucky, always looked 'classy', as she put it. She went out of her way to tell lies so that she could live her life as she wanted. She hid her clothes, applied make-up in the hallway of the flats and removed it before going home, arranged complicated meetings with her boyfriend, which she kept secret from her brothers and everyone in the neighbourhood, and had a bad reputation for no good reason. She turned 17, 18 and then 20, and still nothing changed for her or me. Shadowed all the time like a criminal by her brothers, watched like a hawk by her mother, which added fuel to the flames, Souria wanted just one thing: to have some fun as befitted her age. She paid for her carefree behaviour as I did, but with a forced smile on her lips, not giving a damn about the rest.

I wasn't carefree like Souria. I didn't wear skirts or make-up, or have a boyfriend. My everyday life at home was filled with violence. The first time a boy asked me out because he fancied me, my initial reaction was to slap him. I only knew how to react with violence. 'Who do you take me for?'

My friends gave me a funny look. 'What's up? He didn't do anything wrong; he's cute, nice . . . why did you hit him?'

I was only 14. I felt soiled and humiliated by the boy's proposition; I just saw it as a trap, because I'd heard those words so often: 'Where were you? If I ever see you round the neighbourhood . . . If anyone ever gossips about you . . . If you're not a virgin . . . '

This obsession with virginity, which stopped me having any relationships, even friendships, with boys, was insufferable in 21st-century France, but it became my obsession, one I couldn't shake off. If only I'd known . . .

CHAPTER TWO

Who could I talk to?

I WAS MADE TO be happy and to have fun. I'm quite sure of that and I still don't understand why I didn't have anything like a shred of happiness in my life until the day I finally heard the midwife exclaiming in the corridor of the clinic: 'It's a girl!' A little sister, someone just like me! At first, I didn't believe it. I was sure they were lying. I thought to myself, 'It isn't possible, they'll take her away from me, she's only on loan, I mustn't become attached to her, she won't stick around.' I was 16. I couldn't share very much with her, but I talked to her about my unhappiness, about everything that was going wrong. She was only a few weeks old and already I'd shut myself in the bathroom with her. I'd say, 'Sirinne, I trust you. I can tell you everything and you won't repeat it. I don't know whether it's a good thing that you came into the world, but I'll always be there to protect you. I promise you won't have to live the life I'm living when you're older.'

She became my confidant in all matters. I'd cuddle her and spend so much time with her that we developed an intensely close relationship. I adored her and she felt the same. As she grew older, she didn't seem to mind submitting to paternal authority. If my father said, 'Do this or that,' she did it without protest. Strangely, she obtained what I had never succeeded in obtaining from him: a stable relationship and, as a result, a normal dialogue. This brought me to the conclusion that it was me with my lousy temper who had got it all wrong. Sirinne was able to say 'no' to him about certain things without screaming, unlike me, and she has enjoyed a certain degree of freedom, unlike me. I was locked in an endless father–daughter battle, unable to admit that we were actually both very alike in our stubborn refusal to walk away from this duel based on love and mutual rejection.

I watched my father coming home in the evening, worn out by his 'shitty' job, in the 'shitty' factory, eking out every last penny of his pay to ensure the survival of his tribe. He succeeded – we weren't poor and we weren't rich, like most of the other families in the neighbourhood. I'd have liked him to talk to me about his worries, but he never did. Anyway, he never talked to me about anything. He completely ignored me, especially after that suicide attempt: it was a sin. Suicide isn't 'halal' – it's forbidden by the Koran. When he spoke to me it was either to threaten a beating or to give me the beating itself.

I imagined another language. 'Everything will work out. Your brothers will leave you in peace; they take themselves for royalty. I'm going to make it quite clear that everyone must pull together in a big family. They'll put their things away; they'll clear the table; they'll never hit you again and nor will I. You'll have a room all to yourself and your friends can come round; you'll be able to go out, go into town and to the cinema openly. You're my daughter; I love you and I trust you. You can choose whatever profession appeals to you after your exams and I'll always be proud of you. Later on, if you fall in love with a nice boy and you want to marry him, I'll be happy. And if you're unhappy, you can tell me all about it, always. I'll help you become an independent, happy woman; all I want is for you to be happy.'

It was a dream that would never come true. I was so unhappy and so convinced that he didn't love me that one day I cried out, 'It makes me wonder if I'm really your daughter! Am I?'

Shocked, he gazed at me with tears in his eyes. 'If you're really my daughter? When you were born I held you up to the sky, and said, "You're my sun!" You were my only daughter. I'd like to give you the world! What is it you don't have?'

I couldn't come out with the words I needed to say: 'Papa, I love you, tell me that you love me too and I won't want to die any more.'

My mother merely gave me a lecture. 'It's a sin to want to commit suicide. Why would you want to kill yourself? What is it you don't have? You have all you need; you must remember that many people are far worse off than you. If you commit suicide, you won't go to heaven or hell. Do you want your soul to be lost in limbo?'

I watched my mother absorbed in preparing a tajine stew, telling me off about the washing or the ironing or the vacuuming or mopping the floor when I needed to revise for a maths test. It would have been nice to hear her say to one of her sons, 'Your sister's revising. Since you have nothing better to do, put the dirty washing in the machine and look after your little brothers. Don't let them scream!'

When I was 16 or 17, I'd have also liked her to say, 'If you have a boyfriend, bring him home so that we can meet him.'

My eldest brother was allowed to bring his girlfriend

home. No one thought there was anything wrong with that, so why couldn't I?

I knew the answer to that question. The girlfriend in question was French – in other words, a non-Muslim white girl. She had agreed to convert to Islam so there wasn't a problem, except with regard to her own family, who had kicked her out.

Who could I talk to? The brick wall. My head was a brick wall, so I talked to myself. There were my friends, but most of them had the same problems as me, apart from one who was rolling in it. Her mother and father were executives, and she was free to go into town and to the cinema, free to invite us round, free to have a boyfriend, whom she could talk about openly with her mother.

The first time I entered into a brief romance, I was almost 17 and on holiday in Morocco. He was a little older than me and lived a long way from my neighbourhood back in France. I'd never have gone out with anyone from my town, let alone from my neighbourhood: someone would have ratted on me in a day. He was my first love; we went out together in the strictest secrecy for two summers running. The relationship was doomed to failure anyway, because he was Algerian. I don't make any distinction between an Algerian, a Moroccan, a Tunisian or a Frenchman, but my parents would never have accepted him. A Moroccan girl can only marry a Moroccan boy; he has to be known to the family, the cousin of a cousin or a native of the same small village. Otherwise, it's war. I thought to myself that one day girls would be forced to marry a boy from the same neighbourhood or even the same block of flats and the same floor.

At the age of 17, I hadn't yet kissed a boy. At first, I

sent him off with a flea in his ear as usual, because he was following me in his car. I was walking with one of my cousins and I heard, 'Mademoiselle, I'd like to get to know you . . .'

Using the blunt, abusive language of my neighbourhood, designed to deter any guy trying to pick you up, I retorted, 'Get lost and take your bullshit with you. Have you looked at yourself in the mirror lately?'

While saying that I obviously had to look at him: a dark-haired guy with a matt complexion and emerald-green eyes. I carried on walking while thinking that I was really stupid, and my cousin echoed my thoughts out loud. 'Are you mad? A cute guy like that?'

He followed me all the way, there and back. I lost my temper and at a certain point I even threatened him, saying, 'Will you cut it out? I have ten brothers, so you'd better watch out!'

He laughed, not at all impressed, and on the way home I started to laugh as well with my cousin.

'That guy was really too much! How much time did he waste following me in his car.'

Although I didn't want to admit it, I was flattered, especially as my cousin thought I only attracted 'cute guys' and she didn't.

In Morocco, everyday life was different; the holiday mood, the knowledge that I wasn't being spied on by anyone in the neighbourhood, made me feel a little freer, just a little . . . but I was 17 and the boy was very attractive, well brought up, very relaxed and, most important, he didn't give up easily.

From the balcony of my aunt's house where I was staying during the holidays, I'd watch the little street café where the guys congregated. I had an unrestricted view. He knew I lived opposite and every evening he was waiting there, looking up. And I was always there keeping watch with a supposedly faraway look in my eyes.

One day he sent a messenger to my aunt's house, presenting me with a fait accompli. He had bribed one of my young cousins.

'Leila, some boy is asking for you downstairs.'

'Rubbish! Who is it? Tell him to go and play somewhere else!'

My aunt is elderly and I adore her; she has been living on her own since her divorce. She's a liberated Berber woman with whom I can talk about a great many things.

'Why are you giving him the brush-off like that?'

She went out onto the terrace to look down at the boy standing in front of the block of flats, looking up.

'Have you seen the handsome boy waiting for you downstairs?'

'You know very well it isn't possible. I'm not allowed!'

'What are you waiting for, my poor dear? For your parents to bring you a boy back by force?'

She made me face up to a problem that I'd never really considered before. I knew that arranged marriages existed, but I'd never have believed that my parents would do that to me one day. Not to me – a French girl.

'Believe me, Leila, don't wait for them to bring you back just anyone . . . live your own life.'

She was speaking from experience. Married twice, divorced twice, she had become a lonely old woman of over 70 without any love in her life; she knew much more about it than I did.

I didn't go down immediately, because of my parents. I gave my reply to his messenger, telling him to meet me away from the house. 'Tell him if he isn't there right on time, it's over; he may as well give up!'

When I arrived at our meeting place, he'd already been there for ten minutes.

I felt comfortable with him. He was respectful. Only once did I almost let myself get carried away, but I came to my senses with a start, asking myself what I was doing.

I grabbed my bike and left him in the lurch. I didn't want to see him again after that; I was too afraid of giving in to temptation. For a week, he lay in wait for me in front of the house to speak to me. One day, though, he lost patience and rang my aunt's doorbell.

'You must tell Leila that I want to see her.'

My aunt dreamed up a trap, which was completely unexpected. She said to him, 'Listen, young man, I shan't tell her anything at all. Go to the café and wait for us there quietly. I'll bring her to you and you can sort things out with her!'

All she said to me was, 'Do you fancy buying me a Coke?'

'You want to go to a café at your age?'

'I'm over 70. I don't see why I can't go out for a Coke with my niece for once! Anyway, that café is also a tea-room!'

Women don't go to cafés in Morocco. Young girls go secretly. I wondered whether she hadn't got it into her head to put me to the test, to find out whether I was behaving properly or not . . .

'You really want to go to the café? You're serious?'

'I said I'd like to go there!'

She pulled me by the arm, laughing like a young runaway, and said, 'Come on, get a move on; buy me a drink!'

When I saw who was waiting on the terrace, I realised what my aunt was up to. She pushed me forwards, saying, 'Go on! Off you go! I'll wait here for you.'

She sat down serenely with her Coke and watched us set off to take a stroll with the smug look of someone who had played a trick on the world and his wife.

I explained myself to my lovesick hero, crying, 'I realised I was going to do something stupid that I might regret for the rest of my life. You're a guy, you've got nothing to lose.'

He put his arms around me, and said, 'You're right. I've got nothing to lose and you'd lose a great deal. But if one day we do it, we'll do it by the rules, I promise.'

At least I was sure now that he really loved me since he respected me.

Two summers of stolen moments of happiness, tender kisses and romantic bike rides which I didn't discuss with anyone except my conspiratorial aunt, who was the only person who trusted me and who sincerely hoped that the girls of this new generation were finally going to live their own lives, make their own choices and be happy.

Unfortunately, these brief interludes only lasted during the holidays. The rest of the year it was out of the question for us to contact each other by letter or phone; he knew that as well as I did. The year I turned 18, financial difficulties put paid to a holiday in Morocco. My father was having problems with work and lack of employment, and was forced to find another part-time job. My brothers were costing him a great deal and, apart from one or two who were on income support, the others couldn't do much to help. So I only saw my first love again when everything had already been messed up for me. Too late for love.

At school I had sailed through the first year of the economics/social studies baccalaureate course, and I was now in the second year and had hopes of passing my 'bac'. My father thought I could be 'someone', as he said, although he did nothing but humiliate me on a daily basis, yelling that I was good for nothing at home.

I therefore proved to him that I really was 'a good for nothing', and didn't do a damn thing in the second year of the baccalaureate – or at home. The less I did, obviously the more he insulted me; it was a vicious circle from which there was no escape. As far as he was concerned, being 'good for nothing' had nothing to do with studying, just with submission. He couldn't make me bow my head or give in to him, because he didn't want to understand that all it would have taken was a little love and fairness from him to make me come out on top.

He let his sons get away with murder while his daughter could do nothing right. After he saw my school marks, he could've taken me out of school, kept me at home and condemned me to a life of housework. Instead he enrolled me in a private college as a way of keeping an even tighter rein on me. I was supposed to take a secretarial and accountancy diploma.

From year nine to the moment I had been given careers guidance, my father had made all my decisions for me.

There was a course in social studies there, but that would have meant leaving home, which was out of the question for him. Anyway, he felt I had what I deserved. My academic performance had plummeted so I wasn't able to take the baccalaureate, which would have widened my range of choices. The upshot of this was that I didn't have to make any effort at all for those two years; there was no need to revise since, up to year eleven, I'd always received good marks. I did the continuous assessment assignments standing on my head, obtaining marks between 18 and 20. I was good at French and English, but I hated the idea of becoming an accountant or a secretary stuck in some stuffy office. I wanted to do social work, help other people, come into contact with people, do a job with a human face, instead of spending my time producing columns of figures on a computer screen. I didn't give a damn about a future as a pen pusher that had been decided without any input from me.

I was 18 and I was an adult, wasn't I? Coming of age means nothing to the family. Even when she's married, a daughter is never an adult in the eyes of her father, brothers or husband. My kid brother was always spying on me, and the neighbourhoods' hidden cameras were working overtime. Every evening during Ramadan, I'd go out onto the balcony to smoke my cigarette at the end of the fast. I was still taking risks, playing with fire. Everyone was there; I was in danger of being caught with a fag in my mouth at any moment. My brothers had been trying to catch me out for ages. For a month I'd been smoking my only cigarette of the day in peace and quiet at sunset. So, on the evening before the festival at the end of Ramadan, I was out there enjoying my fag with my mints and my mouth freshener in my pocket in case of any inconvenient spot checks along the lines of 'Open your mouth and breathe in my face!'

I was usually careful to stub out my cigarette butt on the ground and then slip it into the box of matches. I never looked over the edge of the balcony, because someone below might have seen me. That evening I thought my brothers were at football; I was so sure I had nothing to worry about that I casually chucked my cigarette butt over the railing.

But my brothers and their mates were down there and I hadn't heard them. I was wearing bracelets, and the glow of my poorly extinguished cigarette butt and the jangle of bracelets accompanying my gesture gave me away. Instead of staying hidden behind the washing hung out on the balcony, I poked my head over, curious to see where my butt had landed, so 'they' spotted me. One of my brothers looked at me exultantly, as if to say, 'No need to go very far, no need to follow you in the street, I've been trying to catch you out for years and now I've caught you!'

Explanation: if a brother catches his sister disobeying a rule, it gives him the chance to indulge in some vile blackmail.

'I'm begging you, please don't tell Maman and Papa, I'm begging you.'

I even went down on my knees, and said, 'I'm begging you, I'm begging you!'

He didn't say anything to our parents but he made my life a misery for over a month. He'd stretch out on the sofa and click his fingers, saying, 'Hey, fetch me a glass of water!' 'Hey, get my slippers!' 'Hey, do this, do that!'

One day, I was fed up with it, so I answered back and said, 'Sod off!'

What was the worst that could happen? A good hiding? I was used to that; it would just be a little worse than usual, that was all.

'I'd rather you rat on me than go on being your slave. If you want to tell him, then go ahead and tell him!'

'Is that what you really want?'

'Sure, I'd rather have Papa beat me black and blue or murder me, than go on acting like an obedient dog!'

This argument was still going on while I was washing up. He was sure to prefer me as a slave rather than an enemy.

My mother heard raised voices, and said, 'What's going on? Leave your sister alone for a change! You're always on at her!'

'So you think your daughter's a good girl, do you, Maman?'

'She has her faults. But never mind that: leave my daughter alone!'

'What? Your daughter, your daughter, your daughter! Your daughter smokes. Is that what you want to hear? Your daughter smokes fags. I caught her redhanded.'

Then my father's voice cut across us. 'Leila, get into the bedroom! And you! Both of you!'

I've hated that room since I was a little girl. It was behind that closed door that I was attacked by my young abuser or thrashed by my father. I learned the meaning of unhappiness in that wretched room, the only one that could be locked, my parents' bedroom – the room where arguments were settled.

'Have you been smoking?'

I had my brother on one side and my father on the other. If I said 'Yes, I smoke', I'd get a good hiding from my father. If I said 'No', I'd get a thrashing from my brother.

It began with slaps. 'Have you been smoking?' Whack! 'Have you been smoking?' Whack! 'Have you been smoking?' Whack! 'Have you been smoking?' Whack!

I didn't reply. I didn't bow my head, but kept looking straight into my father's eyes, which infuriated him more than anything. My brothers would lower their eyes, but I never did. His blows hurt, but my expression said, 'Hit me if you want, but you won't ever get to me.'

He beat me until my head was swimming and I couldn't see straight, until I finally yelled, on the verge of losing consciousness, 'Yes, I've been smoking. So what? Is that what you want to hear? Yes, I smoke. I'm not as good as you'd like me to be!'

My mother was sitting in the kitchen; she picked up a jug of water and threw the water into my face, followed by the jug.

Then I came in for an even worse beating. They were hitting me as if they were demented, although, strangely, it didn't hurt.

No one ever complains in the neighbourhood. Girls beaten by their parents or brothers obey the law of silence: family honour is at stake. They're so used to it, really, that they think it's normal. If one of these girls dared to complain to a social worker, a teacher or anyone in authority, she'd be shamed. The police don't even come into it. Girls don't consider calling them for a second and I was just like them. Even the slightest temptation to reveal some act of violence in the family is met in advance with a threat: 'If you ever tell anyone, I swear *I'll cut your throat and drink your blood*!'

That's the accepted way of saying it. Even though a Westerner might find this violence hard to believe, we believe it and are convinced that they would cut our throats with as little ceremony as they cut the sheep's throat on the day of the Aid El Kabir festival.

Thus the pathetic business of smoking a cigarette in secret at the age of 18 ended in tears. It didn't have anything to do with protecting my lungs; I wasn't a true smoker in the sense that I was likely to do myself any real harm. An occasional cigarette smoked in secret wasn't going to develop into anything much. As far as they were concerned, it was just a matter of obeying their rules.

A daughter or wife who dares to smoke is labelled a bad girl, the type who frequents nightclubs and who dances in front of men, in other words 'a tart'. However, I would go to any lengths to carry on flouting their rules. I even put my head down the rubbish chute in the kitchen to get rid of the smoke. I refused to let them have complete control over me. By pulling a fast one over them like that, I was relieving much deeper feelings of frustration. With my head down the rubbish chute, I'd think to myself, 'They're in the next room, I'm smoking a cigarette under their very noses and they don't have a clue. They think they're so clever when they forbid everything, but I'm still doing it!' It was a petty sort of revenge.

First thing the next morning, I bought two packets of Virginia cigarettes. I skipped college and in a solitary type of protest, decided to take a walk to my old school.

I never wore my hair loose, but that day the right side of my face was purple with bruises and I'd had to wear it down to cover my cheeks.

I was in a bad way. My friends thought I was acting strangely.

'What's up with you?'

'Nothing! There's nothing wrong with me at all. I just slept badly, I must have flu.'

I was there because I felt as if I needed to confide in someone, but, as always, I clammed up at the first question. No one knew I'd tried to commit suicide when I was 13; no one outside the family knew.

My friends couldn't help me. I'd returned like a nostalgic traveller wanting to breathe in the smell of the baccalaureate, of the illusions I'd lost through my own stupid fault. I was going round and round in circles in my unhappiness. I was almost revelling in it.

I said, 'See you later,' and went to hide at the far end of the enormous school, behind the steps of a building. There, all on my own, I began smoking – one fag, two fags, thinking about my life and talking to myself as usual. 'When all's said and done, you don't know why you stay there. Leila, you're 18, you're an adult, you could clear out, make a life for yourself somewhere else. You're a coward!'

But then there was that little voice that said, 'But if you leave, you'll burn all your bridges with your family. Even if they hurt you, they're still your family. Your family is all you've got.'

I turned it over in my mind for the whole morning – shall I leave, shall I stay – smoking desperately until I made myself cough.

My friend Karim arrived. He was the only one who knew I used to hide there when I was upset.

'What's up, Leila?'

I had my hand against my hair so he wouldn't see.

'Nothing.'

'No? Even that hairstyle isn't like you.'

'I felt like wearing my hair down, just to let it breathe.'

'Stop taking the piss!'

He removed my hand and lifted up my hair to look at my bruise.

At that, I began screaming hysterically. 'What do you want me to say? That my life stinks? I have three solutions, either I kill myself, or I get the hell out of here, or I continue living this shitty life. I smoked a fag, that's all, and my brother ratted on me!'

'Hold on a minute. Have you seen what a state you're in? For a fag? It's just not on!'

'What do you want me to do? If I complain there's the risk that they'll take the little kids away! A broken home, the kids taken into care and the shame of it!'

I didn't want to hurt anyone. I didn't want to break up my family. I wouldn't be able to avoid the shame anyway, whatever happened.

My brothers were also beaten – for example, if one of them came home drunk – but not so much and it wasn't the same. I was beaten for everything. For forgetting something, for a flippant answer, for being late, and I didn't do anything to avoid being hit.

'You won't do anything stupid, will you? Promise?'

'No, don't worry.'

But I had just decided to leave. I didn't tell anyone, not even him. I didn't really know where to go. A friend who wasn't from the neighbourhood somehow managed to find me a hotel for a week, 20-30 miles from home. I'd told him I needed a break, that I couldn't take it any longer at home, although I didn't go into any detail and he didn't ask. Subconsciously, I was afraid that if I began confiding in someone, they wouldn't understand unless I told them *everything*; but I couldn't bring myself to do that, it was too hard, so I kept my mouth firmly shut and that was just as hard.

During my week away I did nothing but cry. I didn't eat; I'd left without taking anything. I didn't even have my identity papers, since my father looked after them. I had nothing with me that would actually let me run away for real. No money, no documents, no place to go. My friend had asked his older brother to pay for my hotel and that couldn't go on for long. He was very nice and really wanted to help me. However, one evening, unfortunately, he wanted to sleep over and I immediately dug my heels in. I hadn't come to ask for that kind of help. He'd understood.

The next day I packed my bags and went home with a

heavy heart. There was no alternative. My escape attempt had failed.

My father, who was completely livid, beside himself with rage and humiliation, didn't even look at me or say a word. I was dead to him. I thought, 'If I open my big mouth, even to justify myself, he'll kill me.'

My mother called me all the names under the sun. 'Where have you been? You're nothing but a tart! Leaving like that! Staying away from home for a week! We don't know what you've done! Tomorrow you're going to the doctor.'

There was never any escape from the humiliation. They took me to the doctor at the age of 18. Even though I was an adult and up to date with my vaccinations, I had to undergo an examination to put their minds at rest.

'Don't worry, she's still a virgin!'

I felt as if I'd been raped. They didn't believe me, or understand me. The only thing that counted was my bloody virginity. They had no respect for me. If someone had said to them, 'But her father beats her! Her brothers beat her, she was quite right to run away,' I'm sure my father, mother and brothers would have chorused in reply, 'Beaten? She said that? How shameful!'

This question of social behaviour, this obsession with virginity, is something I keep turning over in my mind. They drive us crazy with it. I don't have any answers. If I did, I might be able to find some peace of mind. But I don't think there is any logical answer. It's just the traditional rejection of women's independence.

That's the way it is and there's nothing to be done about it. You have to keep walking a straight line, follow the path mapped out for you. Attitudes can't and won't change. Your virginity is the responsibility of your father or brothers, and then of your husband. A woman's body belongs to them. This rightful ownership does your head in. The fathers are placing their honour in the wrong thing, but they refuse to admit it. Their daughters are held under constant suspicion. They search their daughter's thoughts, her personal belongings, her school bag, and her pockets, trying to find any forbidden object. A packet of cigarettes? She's a tart. A powder compact, a tube of mascara or lipstick, red knickers? She's a tart. A note from a boyfriend? She's a tart! A tampon? Straight to the doctor, whether the girl's an adult or not. The pill? She's bound to be repudiated.

'They' also means brothers, cousins, uncles, aunts, mothers-in-law, etc. They don't even treat us like 'objects'. You respect an object, not a woman. This was why I was so angry, why I rebelled. Quite apart from my own particular situation, I know there are thousands of us keeping quiet and being submissive, because they know we can't live without them, outside the family and the community, unless we are 'tarts', as they say. The girls who escape have broken with their families. The girls who climb the social ladder, find jobs and make careers for themselves have come from liberated backgrounds. It doesn't even have anything to do with whether they are second- or third-generation children of immigrants; it's to do with education, culture and a broad-minded attitude towards the modern world.

My father ordered the family not to talk to me. 'I'll thrash the first person who speaks to her!'

He didn't talk to me either. I didn't exist. It didn't bother me too much that my brothers were ignoring me, but the fact that my father was walking past me as if I didn't exist was worse than anything. This silence lasted a month and a half. I counted the days.

My mother only spoke to me when necessary. 'Do this, do that.'

So I didn't go back to college and I resolutely fell ill. I stopped eating; I had a stomach ache. They had to take me to hospital. During this time I couldn't take my exams. No one understood what was happening to me physically. I knew. I was blocked mentally, so my body was expressing my feelings by rejecting what little food I was forced to swallow. No one ever said I was depressed or that it was all in my head. I was just sent home with some medication that was no use at all, firmly resolved to fall ill again.

I wanted to go back to the hospital. I was much better off there, even if it meant driving the doctors up the wall. It was really attention seeking, an attempt to see whether anyone would react and realise that I was in danger at home.

Since the tests revealed nothing, they thought I must have appendicitis. They took me down to the theatre and operated, but my appendix wasn't grumbling about anything. I had a small ovarian cyst; nothing urgent, but while they were there . . .

I enjoyed being a patient. I was in the middle of a nervous breakdown, but I didn't realise it at the time. Like a kid refusing to go to school, I came up with some incredible tricks to stay the centre of attention. For example, I painted a nasty bruise on my ankle with methylene blue. My father took me to hospital, but they couldn't see anything on the X-ray, so they decided it was a sprain. I was in plaster for three weeks and very happy because my brothers were forced to wait on me and sort themselves out.

There always had to be something wrong with my legs, so that I could say to them, 'I can't walk. I can't wait on you any more. I'm useless, so you'll have to do it yourselves.' I must have used the sprained ankle trick three times.

My bad stomach also allowed me to get away with murder – as long as I made them think I also had a temperature. They took care of me again and I couldn't have cared less about the exam when I went back to college. I knew that I only needed one measly mark to pass it and anyway it was my father's choice, not mine.

I was always clashing with my father; he ruled my life, my future. I was tormented by that idea, even in my nightmares. I wanted to escape . . . but where to? I didn't really have the strength to do it, but he was the one who gave it to me one day.

My parents had both gone out. I was supposed to keep an eye on a tajine stew, but I was daydreaming in front of a film on the TV. Naturally, I forgot about the pot and the kitchen filled up with smoke. I scraped off what I could and pathetically recreated the tajine, but there was the smell of burning everywhere.

I looked at the time in despair – my father was going to kill me. He'd told me three times before he left, 'I'm warning you, if something happens while you're supposed to be keeping an eye on the kitchen . . . '

I heard footsteps on the stairs and decided to take the risk and lie. After all, I'd prepared another tajine to more or less the same recipe as my mother's, same vegetables, same meat . . .

'So, you kept a close eye on the meal?'

'Yes.'

'You're sure nothing happened?'

'Of course, what could happen?'

'You're certain?'

'Of course I am.'

He grabbed my head and pushed it into the saucepan.

'Smell that! Do you take me for an idiot?'

He took hold of the broom handle and beat me with it until it broke. He injured my forearm.

I slept all night without complaining. I was aching all over, covered with purple marks and my arm was crooked.

I went to college the next morning, still without saying a word, but the teacher noticed that I was finding it hard to write.

'What happened to you?'

'Nothing, I've hurt myself.'

She wanted to look at my arm; it had swelled to three times its normal size. In the sick room it was still the same official story: I fell over . . .

The nurse called my father and asked him to come into college. He didn't make any comment in front of her; he wasn't even worried, knowing that I wouldn't say anything, but when he drove me to the hospital, he said, 'I'm warning you, if there's nothing wrong with you, I'll break both your arms and this time for real.'

In the car, I prayed, 'Please God, don't let the nurse be wrong . . . Let my arm really be broken!'

I had a dislocated elbow. My arm was put in plaster and it was then that I decided to run away 'for real'. Already, while he'd been beating me, I'd been saying to myself, 'Go on, hit me, because it's the last time.'

My preparations took two or three days. I went to see Martine, a social street worker who knew me, and told her why I'd decided to leave home, still without going into any detail. Even though she was really the only person I trusted completely, I didn't even tell her that my father beat me. I just cried, 'I'm sick to death of it; I can't cope any more . . . I've got to leave; I'm an adult. I'm either going to go mad or top myself, but this time I won't screw it up.'

She understood. It was her job to work things out without asking girls too many questions for fear of antagonising them. Later, she continued to keep tabs on me, intent on saving me from my suicidal impulses and myself. That day she simply asked me if I was really ready and if I had any money.

'I've got absolutely nothing, but I'd rather be homeless than live in that place.'

'But where are you intending to go?'

I had a friend in the south of France who'd said one day in the holidays that I could come and stay with her whenever I wanted. She had a studio flat, a boyfriend and a job, and she was the only one likely to take me in.

I spent the first night in a hostel in the provinces where another street worker took me under her wing and talked to me for a long time, trying to get to the bottom of what was wrong at my parents' place and whether I was really sure of my decision. I was vague. I didn't have the guts to say more, even when my father was miles away and my arm was in plaster. She realised that I'd run off on my own if she probed too deeply. It's so humiliating to be beaten. I should have talked about it, though; I should have told them everything, instead of stubbornly retreating into a destructive silence. With hindsight, I now realise how pigheaded and immature I still was, despite turning 18. The only solution is to agree to talk to someone. It's the only way to avoid making matters worse and finding yourself caught in a trap like me. However, at that time I was like a marionette. My mind kept repeating one phrase over and over: 'I'm unhappy.' End of story. I didn't listen to anyone else, I didn't grab any of the lifelines thrown to me and I was unhappily running around in the belief that

I could cope on my own, which I was totally incapable of doing.

I then had to contact another friend to borrow some money to pay for my flight. My other friend was meeting me at the airport. I hadn't eaten for three days and had hardly slept either; all I had with me was a tiny bag with two sweaters, a spare pair of jeans and my identity card, stolen from my father.

I caught the plane for the first time in my life in Paris – we always drove to Morocco for the holidays. I was exhausted. I felt as if I'd just completed an assault course. I hadn't made any real plans; I just wanted to settle like a tired butterfly at my friend's place. She was a holiday friend, like other acquaintances who also lived in the same neighbourhood, so I wouldn't be a young North African girl lost in a large unfamiliar city. At least I had one landmark: Mina. She was a 20-year-old Algerian, a liberated woman living with her boyfriend – I'd seen them together as a couple on holiday in Morocco. It seemed to me that girls in the south of France were braver than us. Freer.

After that? I had no idea about afterwards. First, I needed a break. I needed to regain my will to live and even to eat; to convince myself that everything would be all right, even if I didn't know how.

I was too naive at that time. I'd never been outside my region, never travelled anywhere other than Morocco or seen anything other than my neighbourhood and the college; I had absolutely no idea how other people lived. I didn't realise how much my parents had been babying me. It was their way of cutting me off from the outside world, of making sure that I could only live under their thumb. If I'd realised that, I might have understood my inability to cope with life more easily and wouldn't have made the mistake of aimlessly running away, of innocently placing my trust in just anyone. Not used to freedom in the outside world, I was seriously at risk, as I was soon to find out.

CHAPTER THREE

A fly

I THOUGHT I WAS determined not to go back to my parents.

I told Mina, who was putting me up, that I was merely on holiday – my arm in plaster was still officially an accident. I was lying to myself and to others; sometimes I felt as if I had a split personality. More often than not, I despised myself deeply for being so cowardly and not facing up to reality. I envied Mina, living with a man without being married, free to let me stay at her place without having to justify herself to anyone. What did she have that I didn't? A strength of character that I most certainly lacked. She was the type of girl who had a 'bad reputation' in my father's view. Still, at least she had an independent lifestyle and I envied her, although I knew I wasn't capable of behaving like her – fortunately for me, it turned out, because my illusions were soon shattered.

At around 9.30 p.m., the evening I arrived, some guys turned up at her place. Mina introduced one of them as her boyfriend, whom I'd already met on holiday, and there were three other guys who looked a little frightening, then two girls arrived and another three boys. I felt uncomfortable right from the start, but wanted to make a good impression, so I answered their questions as politely and evasively as possible. Lying again, as a precaution, to ensure that none of the details mentioned would ever reach the ears of someone who might know me, and that my family would not hear about me on the grapevine, I said I lived in Paris, when virtually the only places I knew there were the Gare de Lyon and now the airport.

The whole gang made themselves comfortable and began to down bottles of beer, chatting loudly. I wasn't used to this type of gathering and suddenly felt in danger. The boys looked every inch what they were, shady inner-city guys strutting around casually to prove they were cool and frightened of nothing. I know their type – the youths in my neighbourhood saunter around with the same deceptively relaxed attitude, but these guys seemed to be part of a gang. At home the boys all know me; we grew up together and I don't have any problems with them. Here I was on unfamiliar ground. I kept watch and remained on my guard. One of them engaged me directly in conversation.

'So, what are you doing here?'

'Just passing through, having a short holiday.'

Everyone was drinking except me. I'd never had a sip of alcohol in my life, and began to freak out big time, watching them go from drinking alcohol to smoking joints. Mina was well aware that I felt completely out of place and frightened in that atmosphere, but I also realised that she wasn't allowed to speak out or stop the drinking binge; her boyfriend was in charge. She did try to calm him down gently, though, saying, 'Hey, I have a friend staying, you might treat her with a little respect.'

He immediately slapped her hard across the face with the back of his hand. Her cheek went purple and she fell silent. I began to feel really scared, but didn't show it. I continued to watch them quietly, always on the lookout. One of the louts sniggered, 'Hey, Mina, what's up with your friend? She's afraid.'

I met his eyes confidently, although my stomach was knotted with fear, and said, 'Rubbish. What makes you think I'm scared? Who do you think you are? I'm from Paris so don't worry about me. The streets are full of little shits like you, and anyway, compared with them, you're nothing!'

Fortunately I'm never at a loss for words. I've always had the gift of the gab. However, my tongue was coping better than my legs, which were starting to tremble. I took refuge in the kitchen to help Mina prepare something to eat. The others were sprawled on the floor with their beers and their joints, waiting to be served. Obviously, whether she was free or not, Mina was stuck in the same system as the rest of us: waiting hand and foot on the men, if you could call them men. Since I couldn't just leave, as I had nowhere to spend the night, I decided to watch TV quietly, while the others continued to knock back the booze. Suddenly I heard some odd noises behind me. Two of the hooligans were playing with pump-action rifles. That clinched it – I was petrified. After all, I didn't really know Mina at all. I had only hung around with her on holiday and hadn't thought she was the sort of person to be mixed up with lunatics, alcohol, joints and guns. I realised she was under the thumb of a nasty piece of work who hit her and controlled her through fear. She'd thought she was doing me a favour by taking me in, but she herself was obviously living constantly under threat. She wasn't working, but getting unemployment benefits. She'd told me that her boyfriend was helping her out financially, but it was clear that this character was probably a drug dealer and that he was lying low at her place with his gang of thugs. I'd only ever seen a pump-action rifle in films. I began to shake inside, while convincing myself that I had to stay calm in front of those idiots. One of the two was obviously showing off, sticking the breech of the gun right under my nose. I confronted him, saying, 'Play with your toy, then; do you honestly think I'll be impressed?'

'Oh yeah, bloody Parisians! Have you heard what you speak like?'

'I speak properly.'

He realised I had character and let it drop, but the other guy zeroed in on me with a smug expression, as if to say, 'I'll try it on with the Parisian bird.'

There was no way he was going to lay a finger on me, but how could I escape from there without injury? I said to myself, 'Leila, you've got off to a bad start here; there are seven guys in this bloody two-room flat, two pump-action rifles lying around, and they've been smoking joints and drinking. There are bottles everywhere; it's a complete pigsty. I'd rather be unhappy at my parents' place than here. What can I do? How can I get out of here? My bag's on the other side of the room; if I try to get it, that moron will block my way.'

I took a deep breath to calm myself and moved back a little, trying to look intently at the television so that the lout would leave me alone but, as I looked round, I noticed a couple lying stretched out on the floor, hard at it right in front of the others. I would never have imagined such a thing could happen. The wide-eyed innocent I was blanched with shame and fright. The smoke from the joints was prickling my nose, the smell of beer was making me feel sick and, surrounded by a gang of hooligans, I was trapped in front of a sordid scene. The girl was quite obviously willing, but what if the character beside me grabbed me with the intention of raping me? Out of my depth and in a panic, I began praying inwardly. 'Where have I landed up, Lord? I'm begging you, Lord, please help me.'

Surreptitiously, I watched the door; it was double-locked and there was no key in the lock.

A couple of yards away the shameless pair had just pulled apart, but the girl remained sprawled on the floor and another boy took the place of the first.

It was dreadful. If I didn't get out immediately, the others were bound to attack me. So I slowly stood up, saying as naturally as possible, 'I'm going to the toilet.'

My hand was shaking as I opened the door to the tiny bathroom. I slid the little bolt shut on the inside and wedged a small bathroom cabinet against the door. I'd rather have died of hunger and thirst in that bathroom than let them touch me.

On the other side of the closed door, a disgustingly vulgar voice leered, 'Oh dear, the girl's freaked out. Hey! Darling! Open the door, open the door for me.'

The good Lord had brought me here to punish me, I was sure of it. I began to talk to Him, sitting on the toilet with my head in my hands. 'You're doing this to punish me, but that's OK, I understand now; I swear I've understood, but please help me, help me escape from this terrible mess.'

The only way out of the flat was the door that opened onto a wide corridor on the fifth floor. I was trapped in a massive block containing hundreds of council flats. There was a window in the lounge, but I couldn't face throwing myself out of it to certain death five floors down except as a last resort.

I'd considered it before locking myself in this tiny room; I'd looked down, saying to myself, 'Never mind, if that bloke attacks me, I'll jump.'

I was more afraid of the possibility of being raped than of the pump-action rifles. It would be unthinkable for me to lose what I'd protected since I was a teenager, my sacred virginity. I would have no choice but to die. Had I run away and left my father for this? He'd been right all along: the outside world was full of danger and God was turning his back on me because I was a bad girl.

I was now crouching on the floor, my back against the cabinet to make my refuge safer, crying silently. Paralysed with fear.

'Open the door for me, come on . . . don't worry, we won't hurt you . . . '

I didn't reply. They didn't hear the sound of my voice even for a second. I was going to die there, in silence, that was the end of it, but I wasn't going to open the door to anyone.

Then I heard Mina's voice (she'd probably been put up to it by her boyfriend), saying, 'Leila . . . come on, it's OK . . . don't worry, come out.'

I replied, 'No, Mina, there's no way I'm coming out.'

'Come out and have a bite to eat.'

'There's no way I'm coming out.'

I stayed there for two nights and a day. Two long nights and an interminable day during which they couldn't take a shower or go to the toilet.

They could've broken down the door, but they didn't, thank God. I'd already been locked in there for several hours that first night and I spent my time alternately sitting on the tiled floor or the toilet seat. I occasionally turned on the tap to splash cold water on my face, because I'd been crying so much from despair and fear. I eventually fell asleep on the tiles, alongside the cabinet, exhausted by listening for the slightest noise, footsteps, laughter. I occasionally started awake when I heard snatches of conversation, Mina's voice: 'You're not being very nice . . . ' and immediately the sound of her being slapped in return. There was only a fairly thin wall between the lounge and the bathroom. I could have counted each of the slaps she took as soon as she tried to negotiate my release from that gang of crazies.

Then I clearly heard Mina's boyfriend's voice ordering her to give him the key.

'The front door's already locked!'

'Yeah, but give me the key anyway. I don't trust you.'

They were afraid that she'd help me to escape and that I'd create problems for them since I'd seen that they had guns.

This time there was really no way out. I'd been thinking that I'd head quietly for the door under cover of darkness and try to open it, but that was hopeless. I was imprisoned in the bathroom and sentenced to death. A tiny hip-bath, a basin, a towel, dirty washing in one corner, the toilet and me, lying in front of the door like a dog. I watched and waited for the silence I'd been hoping for, but they had been living it up all night without stopping. Dawn was breaking and they were still making a din, drinking and smoking as well as the rest, which fortunately I could no longer see.

Suddenly I heard the same man's voice as he banged on the door. 'Come on now, it's OK, come out, don't worry, don't be afraid.'

I didn't reply, but I was screaming inside my head, 'No . . . no . . . no . . . '

There have been times I've been afraid in my life, but never like that. At one point they became really aggressive and another vicious voice yelled, 'It's OK now! Come out, damn it! What's wrong with you? Do you think we're bloody thick or something?'

I kept quiet. Even when Mina tried to persuade me again, I wouldn't say another word. I suspected that the others were egging her on. My head was filled with news flashes. I was the witness on the hit list; I'd seen the guns, the joints, and they'd kill me if I moved. My only defence was my stubborn silence. I couldn't think straight any more or be rational. One thought kept running through my head: 'It's all over for you, say your prayers, it's all over for you, you're dead.'

I was obsessed with the thought: I was dead, whatever happened. If they raped me, my life was over. Whether they assaulted me or just killed me, one way or another I was dead.

I can still see myself sitting on that toilet crying my eyes out. I'd splash my face with water, and then start crying again. I was suffocating in that poky, windowless little room, choking with terror, with powerless tears and lack of air.

I spent the following day in the bathroom. I'd cried so much during the night that in the morning I collapsed. When I woke up I realised that the party was still in full swing and that they were still stoned. A night, a day, another night and another day, stubbornly shut up in that little room with no food, prepared to die. I was slowly becoming paralysed; my mouth could no longer frame the slightest whimper. Even if the emergency services had arrived on the other side of the door, I wouldn't have been able to shout for help.

I was no longer myself in that tiny room; I wasn't there. Another girl was the victim in this nightmare and I was bound to wake up, because none of this could be real. I called myself names in my head, strangely incapable of opening my mouth, as if I'd been struck dumb with terror. 'Why did you do that? You really are thick, you really are useless, and my father is

right when he says I'm thick and calls me a good-for-nothing
. . . I am thick.'

I even stopped breathing so as not to make any noise. On
the other side of the door, there were potential murderers with
guns – a gang high on beer and drugs since Thursday evening.

On Saturday morning, even though I was worn out and
shaky, I decided to venture out, because I couldn't hear any
more noise in the lounge. As far as I could work out, that
meant they'd finally collapsed with exhaustion. It was time to
put everything on the line.

I slowly slid back the cabinet, just enough to open the
door a crack and carefully peep through. They were actually
all asleep, except Mina in the tiny kitchen. She noticed me
and signalled to me not to move. She tiptoed over, slipped
into the bathroom with me and softly closed the door behind
her:

'Don't move from here, I'm going to find the key. I'll say
that I'm going out to buy something or other . . . '

She slipped out, waited until I'd locked the door again, and
then I clearly heard her saying to her boyfriend, 'Hey! Wake
up! Give me the keys! I'm going to buy some croissants for
breakfast. There's nothing to eat in here.'

He mumbled indistinctly, and then everything fell silent
again. I reopened the door of my prison; she was waiting for
me by the front door. As she turned the key once in the lock,
I was behind her, and then I was off, pelting like crazy down
the long corridor in my socks. I hadn't even had time to get
my shoes, my coat or my bag with my identity papers,
money and spare clothes. The bag was in the lounge and I
wasn't taking any risks. Mina left the flat at the same time
as me and caught up with me by the lift. There she began to
cry.

'Leila, I'm so sorry, I didn't want to get you mixed up in this mess.'

'Is this how you live? Tell me? Is this how you live, Mina?'

She didn't reply. This wasn't the Mina of our holidays in the sun with her Moroccan boyfriend, apparently free from all family constraints. She'd believed in that bloke and had fallen into the clutches of a dangerous petty drug dealer with his gang of druggies.

We said our goodbyes in front of the block of flats. She really was going to get croissants for that bunch of losers, and I had no idea where to go because I didn't know my way round the city. I no longer had my things, my money, my papers, but I'd saved my skin. I didn't go very far; just being outside in the fresh air was enough for me at that point, so I sat down on a bench, not far from Mina's flat. There were people around and if they turned up to recapture me by force, I'd only have to scream. Still, I gazed around helplessly. If only I'd taken my address book when I left home, I could've phoned other friends I knew here – Rachid or his cousins Naïma and Mona. Rachid was a nice guy, a divorced man who regularly looked after his son and who had a job; I could've counted on his help. I desperately gazed at a phone box a few yards away. Not only could I not remember any phone numbers, but I also didn't have a penny or a phone card to my name.

I sat there on my own for about ten minutes getting increasingly worked up about forgetting the wretched address book. I was muttering to myself, 'If only someone I know would pass by. You're really thick, you silly girl, there's no chance of that in this city . . . It's huge . . . I'm completely lost here . . . Help me, Lord . . . Make someone pass by . . . '

Suddenly I saw the figure of a boy walking into the phone

box. I couldn't believe my eyes. Rachid? Could that be Rachid? The shame of it if I rushed over there and the boy turned out to be a stranger . . . but what if it was really him and I let him walk away?

I walked closer and walked around the phone box, leaned over to look – it was Rachid! It was a chance in a million that I'd meet someone I knew and I'd bumped into him! Thank you, Lord! I have a guardian angel!

'What on earth are you doing here?'

'I was at Mina's.'

'You were where?'

'At Mina's.'

'Are you out of your mind! Why didn't you call me?'

'I got myself in such a mess . . .'

'I'm not surprised, if you were at her place. Get your things and we'll go.'

'I haven't got my things; everything's still up there.'

'Get in my car and wait for me. I'll go up and get your things. Tell me what there is.'

I only had to wait a few minutes because he didn't take long. The others were furious when he walked in, but Rachid knew them by reputation in the neighbourhood. He calmly announced that he was there to fetch Leila's things.

'How did she get away?'

'Why? Is there a problem?'

'Yeah, there was a bird here, a Parisian bird. Mina unlocked the door for her; I've given her a good beating. She shouldn't have let her get away.'

'She's my cousin.'

'She's your cousin? Mina! Why didn't you say she was his cousin!'

The tone changed immediately. If you're the cousin of a

boy who's known and respected in the neighbourhood, you're protected. No one touches you, it's not done, otherwise there could be reprisals. As a stranger, I was just a 'slut' who was fair game and I'd really been in danger. Mina couldn't help me. Only a man claiming to be part of my family could settle things. It's always down to the men. They're the only ones who can protect you. In this particular instance, though, I was more than happy about it. Rachid was also a holiday friend, but he had nothing in common with that bunch of losers, except that he was from the same neighbourhood. A ghetto neighbourhood, inhabited only by North Africans, with a backdrop of identical, monstrous rows of tower blocks, a maze of soulless streets from which I'd never have escaped on my own.

My neighbourhood was nothing like that. You couldn't describe it as a ghetto.

Having collected my things, Rachid took me to the house of some friends and, on the way, gave me a real dressing down in the car.

'It's completely irresponsible of you to have gone to that girl's place! Everyone knows about that lot! Why didn't you call me? And what on earth are you doing here?'

'I came here for a holiday, that's all. I didn't know Mina lived like that.'

'Now you know!'

I was finally safe with normal people: Rachid's sisters, unproblematic girls living with dependable boyfriends. They all had jobs, nothing with any great future, but they earned an honest wage. With my plaster, my so-called holiday, my unhappy expression and the fact that I tended to burst into tears at the drop of a hat, they soon realised I wasn't on holiday – especially Rachid, whom I knew better. After two weeks he looked me straight in the eye and said, 'Aren't you going to phone your parents?'

'No, yes, don't worry, I already called them.'

'Leila, you're not on holiday! Now tell me the truth. What the hell were you doing at Mina's? No one spends a holiday at her place!'

I didn't want to admit that I'd decided to call Mina a little by chance, but particularly because she wasn't Moroccan and so no one from my community would know where I was. So I began to cry, which got me out of talking. He didn't press the point.

'OK, let's drop the subject for the time being. We'll all go for a walk together, that will take your mind off things.'

I had lost my appetite and was losing weight; if my parents were suffering because they had no news, I think I was suffering three times more. I spent most of my time in tears. My friends could see I was upset; I couldn't hide my situation from them any more; I had the word 'runaway' stamped on my forehead. As I still wouldn't talk about it, they didn't leave me alone for a minute. They took turns at trying to catch me out.

'Leila, you're unhappy, but your parents are bound to be unhappy as well. You must phone them. What's wrong?'

'I've had enough, that's all.'

'And we've had enough of watching you cry. We're doing everything we can and it's no use. You have to phone them.'

'Not now.'

So Rachid and his friend dragged me forcibly to the phone box, gave me a phone card and shut me inside.

'You're not coming out until you phone your parents to reassure them and make yourself feel better.'

I screamed at them. I was still afraid of my parents, and

even more so because I'd left home over a fortnight ago, this time without giving them any sign that I was still alive. What could I say to my father without him cursing me? To my mother without her begging me to come home?

On the other hand, upsetting them was upsetting me. I had thought I was putting a great deal of distance between us by taking refuge with an Algerian woman. How stupid can you be? The community was always there and my friends knew very well that a North African girl without a diploma and without any family to turn to, even at 18, was incapable of surviving unscathed. I felt like a panic-stricken fly trapped under a jar. It becomes agitated, tries to climb towards an illusory way out above it, and then slips down the side and falls. In that phone box, I was the fly and I was trapped.

Rachid and his friend only wanted the best for me. They were right. I was incapable, like so many other girls, of escaping from the family home. They also didn't know my story, because I still wouldn't talk about it – and even if I had confided in them, they would probably have replied, 'OK, so you've been roughed up a little, but so what? They're still your parents . . . '

Just yelling 'I've had enough' wasn't enough of an explanation for them. I'd also said 'I've had enough' after trying to commit suicide at the age of 13. I've said it hundreds of times. I couldn't open up any more than that.

So, convinced they were doing me a favour, and they'd already done me one by protecting me, my two friends wedged the door of the phone box shut – two stubborn backs, two walls, unashamedly turning away anyone wanting to use the telephone.

'Occupied! Try somewhere else.'

They left me in there for nearly three hours. I sat on the

ground; they sat on the ground on the other side. After a time I didn't know whether to laugh or cry.

'Open the door, don't be mean.'

'No'.

'Suit yourselves. I'm perfectly happy in here, anyway. I've got two bodyguards, and I'm in no danger.'

'That's what you think! We might leave you in there all night – wedge the door shut and go have ourselves a party somewhere. It's better than Mina's bathroom, though – at least you can look out.'

By talking nonsense, making me giggle and then making me cry, they managed to coax me into lifting the phone off the hook.

I was overcome with fear. What was I going to say? The only thing that made me feel better was the knowledge that my father wouldn't be at home at that time of the day.

There is no life outside your family, your clan, without your parents or the protection of a man. In Europe, a white French, Swiss or Belgian woman who runs away from her parents at the age of 18 has other resources. There are hostels. She simply has to go to the cops and say that her father or brother is beating her; she can bring things to a head without worrying too much. As far as we're concerned or, at any rate, in the Moroccan community, girls don't consider denouncing their family for a second. No one else understands how shameful that would be. It eats away at us; we regard ourselves as cowards, we struggle clumsily and finally we give in, because there isn't anywhere else to take refuge. I had arrived back at square one.

I gazed at that blue telephone, which was completely impervious to my panic, and I found it hard to pick up the receiver. I tried three times to call. The first time I let it ring once and then hung up. The second time it rang twice before I hung up. The third time I heard my mother's voice. 'Hello, hello, is that you, Leila?'

I froze. She'd immediately thought of me.

'Hello, Leila, please talk to me, my girl, I'm begging you. Tell me it's you; tell me that you're alive. Leila?'

I was crying and she heard me sobbing. I managed to say, 'Yes, Maman, it's me.'

'Where are you, where are you? Wherever you are, we'll come and get you!'

'No, no, I'm not telling you, it's not worth it.'

'But where are you? Tell me so that I'll at least feel better!'

'Don't worry, everything's OK now, I'm with a family, I'm OK.'

I quickly replaced the receiver, after promising to call back.

My friends opened the door triumphantly: they'd won. Actually, I did feel relieved at having put my mother's mind at rest, but I hadn't decided to go home. I guessed my father would be furious that I hadn't told them where I was and he'd be thinking all kinds of sordid things about me – for example, that I might be with some man, of course. Having had his authority flouted, I thought about the lies he must have been forced to tell to explain my absence in the neighbourhood, without endangering 'his' honour and 'my' reputation. The guilt I felt constantly was even stronger when I was far away from him.

I was probably going to slink home of my own accord with my tail between my legs. He would almost certainly let me in, but morally he'd leave me standing out in the cold. No psychology, no affection, just tradition – that bloody authoritarian tradition which silences rebels. I was guilty of lack of respect, of running away, of dishonour and God knows what else.

I felt ill, on the verge of hysteria for some strange reason. I felt as if I needed to laugh so I wouldn't cry any more, and I was laughing too loudly; I was talking too loudly about nothing. The girls thought I felt relieved so they decided to take me into town to let my hair down. Only in moderation, though – we were just going out of the neighbourhood one evening to have a Coke in a café in the city centre.

It must have been about 10 p.m. Everything was fine until we walked past the terrace of a café and I immediately noticed a strange, heavily made-up, common-looking girl showing a great deal of cleavage and wearing an extremely short skirt that looked more like a belt. I'd never seen a prostitute before. I felt as if I were on Mars. My friends weren't shocked, though.

'It's no big deal, the red-light district's over there.'

I don't know why I was so shocked, but before I had time to discuss it with them, a man overtook us and as he walked past he smacked my bottom. He did the same to my friend. I screamed and immediately began to shake all over. Then I fainted and woke up in hospital.

The doctor questioned me for a long time. I had haemorrhaged; I'd started my period suddenly and abnormally.

'Have you ever had this type of problem before?'

'No.'

'Is everything OK in your life? Tell me about it.'

'It's fine. I'm on holiday; there's nothing to tell.'

'You realise that this type of thing is a nervous complaint, don't you? Are you sure everything's OK? No stress? Have you ever had spasmophilia, epilepsy or tetany?'

'No, never. I'm fine.'

'Not in my opinion. Have you been losing weight? A lot?'

'No, not very much.'

I was lying; I was as scrawny as a chicken in a Moroccan village. I wasn't eating and was sleeping badly. It was probably obvious to the trained eye of a doctor, and you don't faint because some idiot smacked you on the bottom or because you'd seen a whore for the first time.

I didn't say a word; I didn't take advantage of the situation to ask for help at last. Nothing. Somewhere deep inside, buried in my brain, I guessed that the silence imposed on my chaotic life – my traumatic childhood, the beatings, my father – was poisoning my mind, and that from time to time my body did what it could to call for help. However, the time still hadn't come for me to analyse all this. Paradoxically, it was only this silence about my problems that enabled me to keep going – if I'd talked about them, I would have collapsed.

I didn't make the connection between my fear of rape, my obsession with my virginity, the sight of a prostitute and an insulting slap on the bottom. If someone had tried to explain it to me, I'd have laughed in their face. I could always laugh at my bad experiences, except about the most serious things, which I never mentioned. Hysterical, me? Yes, so what?

'Everything's fine . . . I'm on holiday.'

A wide smile for the doctor, a fit of the giggles with my friend and I managed to sidestep all their questions. But I was at the end of my tether and I was afraid something really serious might happen to me.

I called my mother back to tell her I wanted to come home, but that I didn't have any money left. She asked me for an address where she could send me some money. Then I was on the plane home, humiliated by yet another failure. My breaks for freedom were really pathetic.

I thought I'd had a taste of hell away from my family, but I was going straight back into the lion's den by returning home. I don't know whether it was then that my father began thinking about marrying me off. The idea must have occurred to him; he had to make sure I was still a virgin again. I was going to turn 19 later on in the year, I had dashed his 'ambitions' for accountancy, I had been a disappointment in every way and he must have thought about getting shot of me one way or another. I had never considered an arranged marriage, though. I was too busy feeling unhappy, too busy suffering, and coming home was like being put back in prison – that was quite enough to think about.

My mother hugged me tightly, and said, 'Thank God, you're safe and sound.'

My father wasn't back from work yet. My brothers didn't say a word. I realised that, as usual, the head of the family had issued his orders with regard to me. 'Don't ask her any questions. Don't speak to her.'

When he came in, I said 'hello', but he didn't answer. Once again, I didn't exist. I wanted to curl up and die when he did that to me. I'd rather be beaten than be ignored so completely. It really upset me; he couldn't have imagined how much.

My father's favourite phrase when talking about me was: 'I'd rather have had 100 boys to raise than just one girl.'

I didn't take the BEP diploma, but my father didn't let the matter drop; he was determined that I should sit the exam as an independent candidate.

I thought, 'To hell with you. I won't take it,' and said out loud, 'Yes, sure, I'll take it when I go back to college in the autumn. I've found out all about it. Don't worry, enrolment isn't until September.' I was plotting again. You'll lie all the time for a little freedom. You're even prepared to swear on the Koran. God forgive me, I've sworn on it thousands of times. I preferred to lie and swear on the Koran so that they'd believe me just a little, rather than get another thrashing.

I had promised to take the exam but, at the same time, I didn't feel able to stay at home. I needed a job, anything; even the most dead-end position would be a breath of fresh air and make me financially independent. So I registered with the temping agencies. I plagued them on the telephone and visited them twice a day in case they forgot about me. Occasionally I telephoned even before they'd had time to turn on their computers. I wanted to be first in line for the first opportunity.

Even if it meant sweeping up somewhere, I couldn't bear staying at home any more. Eventually I found some assembly-line work in a factory. Nothing wonderful; my father would have liked to shut me away in an office – that was his idea of success – but I no longer had any big ideas. I didn't give a damn about my future. The important thing was to keep going, to hold out on a day-to-day basis, despite opposition from him. So I started bringing in a substantial income, which he couldn't turn down while waiting for me to take the BEP as an independent candidate.

By a stroke of luck, I was soon offered some night work from 9 p.m. to 5 a.m., which doubled my pay. I said yes on the spot, but how was I going to get my parents to agree to that? A daughter doing night work!

I began with my mother. 'I'm warning you right away that from tomorrow I have to work from 9 p.m. to 5 a.m., otherwise I'll get the sack!'

Another lie.

'But your father won't stand for that!'

'Either I continue working or I lose my job and let someone else take my place.'

A fly

My father obviously grumbled. A girl doesn't run around on her own at night.

'You can drive me there in the evening and then collect me at 5 a.m. That way you'll see that I'm working and that I'm not hanging about in some nightclub!'

Actually, there was a nightclub in that outlying neighbourhood and I'd never yet set foot in such a place. I wanted to, just to see what it was like and to defy another taboo. At first my father scrupulously gave me a lift there and back, but I knew he'd get tired of it and that I'd be able to lie about working extra hours so that I could visit that den of iniquity once or twice with some friends.

I obviously had to sleep during the day. That didn't stop anyone giving me housework to do. I could hear shouting and doors slamming, and my brothers walked in and out of the room with no respect for my sleep at all, which sometimes drove me crazy. There were four of us in each bedroom, three brothers in 'mine', so it was impossible to be alone I had been putting up with living at such close quarters since I was a kid, but it was becoming increasingly intolerable. It had been one of my dearest dreams to have a room of my own, even if it was a tiny box room. At 19, most girls of my age had their own rooms, their own chests of drawers, their privacy, even if it was only limited.

I have always had to put up with violations of my privacy. They used to dig through my school bag, my handbag and my mind, and now no one gave a damn about my sleep. As a result, even when I'd woken up I pretended to be asleep. I'd go to bed at 6 a.m., they'd get up at 7 a.m. to go to school and at 10 a.m. at the weekend; I could hope for some rest after that. The worst times were the weekends and holidays, so I worked extra hours at the weekend to earn more and, more importantly, to spend as little time at home as possible. During my years at school and college, my parents had known how I spent my time there, or thought they had, but I'd been lying: occasionally I hadn't had lessons in the afternoon and my real time wasn't as well structured as it appeared on paper. This allowed me to acquire a few hours of freedom here and there.

Now I was also lying about my pay. I gave some to my father, but didn't tell him exactly what I was earning. I carefully hid my payslips in my locker at the factory. However, since I had to have a bank account, my father kept my bankcard at home. 'You don't need your card to go to work!'

He had my pin and as soon as he needed money he would use it, as would my eldest brother. He even used my card without warning to buy one of his girlfriends a gift.

By working like mad, I was earning 12,000 francs a month but, despite all my efforts, I could never save 1,000 francs. I could've taken my driving test and scraped enough together to buy a little car, but it would never have been just mine. My brothers would have immediately taken advantage of it. I gave up that idea.

I was almost 20. I was continuing to live an apparently peaceful life and finally managed to go to a disco with my friend Souria, with the help of another friend, the sort of guy you'd say was like a big brother. We could trust him to escort us: he didn't give a damn what we did, since we weren't his sisters.

The nightclub was awful. Noisy, smoky and nearly everyone was pissed. I didn't like the atmosphere. I was disappointed and uncomfortable. We sat there like two country cousins who'd just come into the big city to observe the nightlife. Souria is pretty, blonde and light-skinned. She looks nothing like a North African, and I always tell her that she's lucky. Because of her appearance she can get into town more easily; people who don't know her think she's French and leave her alone. She was chatted up that evening, though, which we thought was very funny.

I didn't dance, as I couldn't bear the feeling that people were looking at me, and nor did Souria. We felt more as if we were in a zoo watching some unfamiliar wild animals. But we were there. We'd done it.

On the journey back I was still afraid that something might happen, like an accident, and that the police would tell my parents. That had happened to a student friend of mine who was staying in lodgings a long way from home. She had claimed that she had to revise for mid-term exams and wasn't able to come home one weekend during Ramadan. That evening she'd decided to go to a nightclub and that was the night that fate intervened. She was killed in a car accident on the way. I thought about her in silence; what if I died in an accident like that? What if I survived? How would I explain?

Life was an adventure, an obstacle course and non-stop lies. Souria had decided, for example, to have her ears pierced at the same time as me. As far as the family is concerned, it's traditional to have a hole in your ear, and North African girls wear earrings almost from birth. However, the adventure this time was to have two extra holes, so that we could wear three earrings. We talked about it for a fortnight before deciding. Three holes is body piercing and exclusively reserved for bad girls, like cigarettes and discos.

Finally our minds were made up. Neither of us would have done it on our own. When we were at the ear-piercing salon, we both swore not to abandon the other.

'You won't run off?'

'I swear! On my life, on the Koran!'

If the second hole was unbearable, the third was terrible. We came out with our ears bright red and burning, but giggling nervously. I knew I was going to get the shit knocked out of me if my father noticed. Souria had the hiccups.

'You know we're going to be beaten black and blue and you're laughing!'

'What do you want me to do? Cry before it happens? We've done something really stupid. We have to come to terms with it and see it through to the end.'

Sitting on a bench with our ears on fire, we watched the world go by in the middle of the neighbourhood, doubled up with laughter.

'Look at that guy, he thinks he's so handsome, he looks more like a country bumpkin.'

Having our ears pierced like that was a serious act of provocation and I was afraid, but whenever I was afraid I dissolved into fits of giggles that set other people off, and so did Souria. It was a psychological release that was essential in our narrow lives. We had to go home, however, and at that point neither of us thought it so funny, even if joking was still the done thing. 'Bye, Souria. We'll see each other again in the next world, perhaps in Heaven.'

I managed to hide my ears longer than she did. I put on a headscarf, which I usually didn't wear. My mother didn't ask any questions; she just thought I was imitating her. Souria was caught by her mother after two days. She pulled her hair and kicked her from pillar to post, saying, 'Look at the state of you! What does having three holes say about you? You should have had your nose pierced while you were at it!'

Naturally she called her a tart and Souria phoned me to tell me all about it, and my mother answered the phone. In such situations, it's extremely important to follow what we called the 'accepted etiquette'; above all, it's essential not to offend your friend's mother in case she forbids you to see each other again. The preliminary greetings are very important.

'Hello? How are you? How are the children? How are you keeping? And how is grandmother back home? Say hello to her from me and to your brothers and all the family . . . ' – a typical conversation before my mother finally passed me the phone.

'So you still haven't been caught! Swear to me on your mother's life that you haven't been caught! How have you managed?'

'I've put a scarf over my head.'

'You're wearing a headscarf!'

She hadn't thought of it; and you had to keep the studs in for at least a month for them to heal.

Eventually, one day, I was found out as well. I wasn't wearing the scarf any more. I just wore my hair loose to hide my ears. I was serving food at the table. My father looked at me.

'What have you got in your ears?'

'Nothing . . . '

'Lift up your hair.'

My mother screamed shrilly but, oddly enough, I didn't get a beating that time.

'You poor girl, you'll drive me to despair.'

I was bringing my pay home. I paid the rent and never hesitated to give them extra money. I had bought my peace and, although I still received the odd slap, it became increasingly rare and the broom handle stayed in the cupboard.

Souria was beaten black and blue as she had been when she was a teenager. She was even hit by her sisters, model daughters who didn't show their faces in public, not even on the balcony, and had remained as pure as the driven snow until their marriage. They couldn't understand why Souria was so different from the rest of the family.

As for me, I dressed to avoid drawing attention to myself. I didn't wear too much make-up, and it was always very discreet. Souria was the opposite: tall, slender and blond, with blue eyes, always using make-up and wearing figure-hugging jeans. She was very pretty and flirtatious, which made her life hell in the family home, but gave her greater freedom of movement outside. No one took her for a North African.

At that time, there were three of us, inseparable friends who were the same age: Leila, Souria and Nadia.

Nadia ran away from home overnight. Her parents were *hadj* – they'd made the trip to Mecca. She came from a family of four boys and three girls. The eldest daughter had capitulated: married by force to a boy from back home in Morocco, she now wears a headscarf. Her parents had found a photo of her at the swimming pool, wearing a bathing costume, a 'disgrace' that was the reason behind the marriage. The middle daughter was going out with a boy; they were openly in love and wanted to get married, but the parents didn't get on.

The boy's mother said to the girl's mother, 'My son will never take your daughter, because she's a tart; she doesn't cover herself up when she's with him!'

The girl's mother retorted, 'Your son's already ancient history; there's no way he'll ever marry her!'

Nadia vanished into thin air. I saw her again once – she's gained her freedom but at what cost. She isn't married, but has a child and has broken off all contact with her family.

We often talked about these tales of forced marriage.

'Did you hear that Khadîdja married a complete stranger

from back home! The girl who said she'd never marry a guy from Morocco has ended up doing just that!'

'As for me, anyway, no way, never, never, never!'

'Can you imagine? Making love to a complete stranger, you, the girl who guards her virginity like crazy!'

'No way . . . I'd run away or I'd die!'

We discussed it like kids. We ridiculed forced marriages as if they were in some TV soap like *The Young and the Restless*. Letting our imagination run wild together was our way of keeping reality at bay.

Summer arrived. I couldn't go on holiday because I was working for the whole month. I gave them money for the trip because my father was skint, but I wasn't allowed to stay at home by myself. Two brothers were there to make sure I behaved: the eldest, who still lived at home, and the one who'd been my parents' surveillance camera for so long and who regularly caught me out, smoking.

One day I caught him smoking in the toilet, the guy who was always pretending to be a saint. He'd even acquired a taste for smoking joints. In front of my parents, however, he was the model brother.

'Are you going to breathe in my face now?'

'Yes, I'm smoking, so what?'

'So nothing! I'll tell you one thing: I'm going out onto the balcony to smoke a cigarette since I can do so openly for once and, if you open your big mouth, I promise you that if I die, so will you!'

After that, we became accomplices. He even came to the nightclub with me that year. I made the most of that last summer of freedom to live it up a little. I was the one with a death wish in the family – I had to experiment as much as possible, and needed to live life to the full. Mind you, that wouldn't be very much for a young white girl of my age: three holes in my ears, a trip to the seaside, half a dozen evenings in a nightclub where I didn't flirt or dance, and a ride at the funfair, which was also one of the things forbidden by my father. I loved the roller coaster. It made me feel completely free, as if I was floating above everything. Why we were forbidden to go on fairground rides is a mystery to me.

I made the most of this holiday without my parents on my back, even if I was working. It was as if I were living the last days of my life. The TV remote all to myself also represented freedom. The only time I'd been able to watch TV on my own was the day I burned the tajine. I was intoxicated by this unfamiliar freedom. I even went so far as to have my hair cut short.

Souria was sceptical, and said, 'Aren't you scared?'

'I'll get a beating, but what's done is done. I won't be able to stick it back on!'

I even treated myself to a classy hairdresser and paid a small fortune. I didn't recognise myself. With sleek, shoulder-length hair, I suddenly looked like a real girl.

However, when my parents came back, my father thrashed the living daylights out of me, and my mother pulled my hair with indignant screams. Traditionally, you're not allowed to wear your hair down, so even when it was cut short, I wore it up. You do see girls with short hair around here, but everyone's mother despises them. 'Look at her over there, she looks like a man!'

Hair symbolises the woman and the woman's body is in itself an offence. I never wore a headscarf (except to conceal the holes in my ears), and I don't understand the girls who wear one now when their mothers have given up wearing them. Everything is paradoxical. You must have long hair, but you must wear it up or hide it, and when you have it cut, you must still keep it to a standard length. Although I finally allowed mine to grow out, it certainly wasn't out of obedience, but because I couldn't afford to go to the hairdresser that often.

Everything seemed to be going well the summer I was 20 but, strangely enough, I said to Souria, 'I have a bad premonition.'

'A premonition of what?'

I didn't honestly know. It was a vague feeling. Perhaps I knew my freedom was only temporary and that nothing would be the same when my parents came back. I was 20, I had a job and I was certainly not thinking about marriage. No one mentioned it, and anyway, I'd vowed that I wouldn't let anyone have me.

One day my father phoned from Morocco to give me all the news, and said, 'I'll hand you over to your mother.'

Once etiquette had been observed and I'd been given all the family news, she said, 'Leila, my girl! Guess who came to visit us?'

'I have no idea; anyway, everyone descends on you as soon as you get there. They live "free" for a month.'

'Your uncle came! With your cousin too.'

'Which cousin?'

'Abdel!'

'Oh, OK.'

I knew him by name, that was all, and I really couldn't have cared less.

'But he didn't come alone.'

'Oh.'

'He came with a friend who lives in Spain. Moussa.'

'So what?'

'He's a very nice boy.'

I still didn't see what was coming.

'You know, Leila, you're old enough to get married. Quite a few suitors are coming to ask for your hand in marriage.'

'Listen, Maman, stop right there! There's no way I'm having a suitor who turns up when I'm not there and whom I've never met! That's not for me. Anyway, I'm too young, I've only just started work; I don't have a steady job. Absolutely no way!'

'OK, OK, fine.'

All kinds of plots were being hatched over there without my knowledge. Strangely enough, though, I didn't make the connection between my premonition and that conversation. I didn't think my parents would go that far. I was French, I'd been born in France, I now had my national identity card, I'd come of age two years ago, I was working and I hoped one day I'd be brave enough to live on my own in a little studio flat, not far from my family, but on my own.

What I didn't know was that I was now ideal prey for any Moroccan bachelor who dreamed of settling in France. I still hadn't realised that this was such a huge market, a perfectly legal bona fide organisation.

I was no longer a fly trapped beneath a glass; this fly was now caught in a hellish spider's web.

CHAPTER FOUR

An end to love stories

My mother began taking me to wedding ceremonies when I was about 15, issuing the usual orders. 'I'm warning you, you'd better not move from your chair. Stay close to me, I don't want you dancing, I don't want this, I don't want that . . . '

Wedding ceremonies are an opportunity to make a tally of the marriageable girls. The mothers and mothers-in-law handle everything. The fathers are usually on the other side of a curtain, keeping an eye on the dance floor to make remarks of crucial importance.

'Look at that girl over there! She's been on the dance floor since the evening began, trying to draw attention to herself!'

'Look at Moulay's daughter; she's sitting quietly with her mother.'

It's like a free catalogue. On one side, there are the bad girls, and on the other, the marriageable ones.

I could have acted like a bad girl and drawn attention to myself to avoid being married off to just anyone. However, on the one hand, I'd have been beaten, and on the other, I didn't suspect anything. Besides, it's not in my nature to draw attention to myself. I would clown around in secret with my friends, but in public I was shy and reserved.

A Moroccan wedding is beautiful, magnificent, but sometimes there's also the other side of the coin. The negotiations are handled mainly by the women. There are matchmakers, who are fairly easy to spot – aunts or distant cousins who act as go-betweens. If a boy back home in Morocco is keen to get married because he needs papers, but has no direct contact with families in France, he'll ask one of these woman to act as a go-between and find him a girl from a good family in France.

Souria, carefree as always, paid more attention to boys at weddings than I did. She would have liked me to find a boyfriend like hers. At one particular wedding party, she said:

'I'm telling you, there's some hot stuff here.'

'All the better for you.'

'Give me a break! Think about yourself for once.'

'I'm not here for that. I'm not interested.'

A friend of my brother's called over to me. My mother knew him, so I was able to stop for a few minutes to chat with him without getting a black mark against my name. Another boy walked over and joined in the conversation. He was handsome, but I'd never seen him before. On principle, you shouldn't talk to boys who aren't known by the family.

My mother was already staring at me. I tried to talk just to my friend, my head resolutely turned towards him, but the other guy persisted.

'So you work nights?'

'Yes.'

'Is your family OK with you working night shifts?'

'For the time being, yes. I can earn more that way and get some peace and quiet, and it leaves my days free.'

'You're not married?'

'No, I'm not married.'

This time, I sensed my mother looking daggers at me, so I cut the conversation short.

'It was a pleasure to meet you. My name is Kader.'

'I'm Leila.'

The way he addressed me directly at a party caused serious problems. When your parents or the community are around, you must lower your eyes and walk away. I should have left him standing there, without answering. The girls in the kitchen were already looking at me. Not only that, but I'd talked to two boys at the same time and my 'reputation' was beginning to be soured by the fact that I was a smoker. I was verging on more than impertinence.

My brother's friend tried to reassure me, saying, 'Don't worry, he's my cousin.'

And to Kader: 'She's the sister of a very good friend of mine, she comes from a very good family.'

You always have to specify the origins, the family, the label, and the trademark. You say a 'good family' straight away. Translation: 'marriageable'. Otherwise you don't say anything at all – it's a silent code, whose translation means 'Don't even think about anything serious', under the possible heading 'It's down to you'.

Abdou was very fond of me; he respected me as his best friend's sister. He also knew that although I was always shooting my mouth off, I wasn't actually seeing anyone.

I was unintentionally sensible when rejecting boys; it wasn't that I was agreeing with my parents. I just didn't want to put myself in a situation that was likely to cause me more problems than I already had. It was the only way of keeping my virginity safe. I was too afraid of falling in love with someone, of losing control and letting him go all the way, and then risk things ending badly. If I got to that point, my parents would have won: I would really be a tart. Anyway, I wasn't ready. My childhood hadn't allowed me to develop. I automatically distrusted all boys; as far as I was concerned, they were all the same – that's to say, cowardly and dangerous. I therefore forbade myself to fall in love. No one was going to marry me or go out with me.

Abdou handled the situation as normal so that his cousin knew whom he was talking to. I hurried away, but my mother called me over.

'Leila! Who were you with over there?'

'I was with Abdou! You know him!'

'Yes, but who was the other boy?'

'His cousin. I was talking to Abdou, Maman, not to the other boy.'

She looked at me suspiciously, and said, 'Go and sit down and stay put.'

At weddings, you're supposed to sit down and watch and wait, so I sat down. I watched the girl getting married to a boy who would obtain 'his papers' through her. Everyone knew what was going on. This must have been the fourth wedding of this type that I'd attended. It was a rather sad formality, all the same. There are happy weddings too, fortunately, but I doubt whether there are proportionately more of them.

Kader had sat down opposite me and I was conspicuously ignoring him, despite Souria nudging me with her elbow, and saying, 'He's the best-looking guy here this evening and he's yours. I promise you! He hasn't taken his eyes off you.'

I wasn't interested in the guy's looks, even though all the

girls were watching him. It was rather awkward trying to look indifferent all the time. I particularly didn't want to meet his eyes; it was essential that he didn't think I was interested in him.

I don't really understand why I was so uncompromising. On the one hand, I dreamed of falling madly in love with someone I'd met and kept hoping it might happen. I was expecting that a man would miraculously appear before me and that I'd no longer be able to control myself. On the other hand, I forced myself to treat boys with an aggressive chilliness. Kader acted shrewdly.

My father had gone and only Abdou was worthy of seeing us home, so my mother sent me to find him, but he replied kindly, 'I must take my mother and sisters home first. I'll be back in ten to fifteen minutes!'

Kader seized this opportunity and offered his services as a driver.

I went to inform my mother of his offer. Abdou added, 'Don't worry, Aunt, he's my cousin. He'll take you home.'

I wasn't surprised that my mother accepted. As my 'eldest brother's best friend's cousin . . . ', Kader was completely respectable.

That was how he found out where I lived, and several days later, at the market, Abdou spoke to me.

'Leila, Leila, I must talk to you. I've been looking for you for ages. My cousin Kader has really fallen for you. I shouldn't tell you that, but he's desperate to meet you!'

I was stunned. I said, 'Abdou, why are you doing this to me? You've got a nerve saying that your cousin's fallen for me. That's crazy. Who does he take me for?'

'Hold on! I told him you were a girl from a good family; he'll treat you with respect!'

'We'll see.'

He gave me his cousin's phone number, and said, 'Call him.'

Souria was over the moon. 'What are you going to do?'

'I'm not calling him.'

'You're not calling him? Why won't you call him? You've seen the guy, haven't you? He's got a job and he's cute. Leila, what harm would it do to have a coffee with the guy? Having a cup of coffee doesn't mean he's immediately going to grab you and start kissing you!'

'I don't trust guys. You know what trust means? It means you end up falling into a trap that's almost impossible to escape from.'

'Give me a break! You're just scared!'

She managed to convince me in the end.

I wanted to give it a go, but only to prove to her that I wasn't scared, while hoping that something might happen, that my suitor might do something, anything, that would justify sending him off with a flea in his ear. That would be one way of shutting my friend up. 'I told you so, I was right, he's a fool.'

So I didn't call him the next day. He was the one who called me. He'd nagged his cousin so much that he'd given him my number with strict instructions about what to say if my mother answered the phone.

'Hello, Madame, this is Company X calling, I wanted to talk to our temp, Mademoiselle Leila Z . . . '

When my mother handed me the receiver, I heard him say in a rush, 'Hello, it's Kader. I'd like to see you again. Would you like to have a coffee with me?'

After a short silence, having made sure that my mother was busy chatting to the neighbour on the landing, I claimed it was too late, that I was about to leave for work.

'Come on, give me break! Pull the other one! You start at 9 o'clock in the evening and it's 3 o'clock in the afternoon; you're not telling me you need as long as that?'

'I need time to surface. I'm still tired, we went to bed late.'

'Anyway, I know where you live; if you don't want me to turn up and wait for you in front of your block of flats, then say yes!'

I finally agreed to meet him on neutral territory: a place frequented by visibly non-Muslim white people.

I wore really scruffy clothes to put him off. An old track-suit, tatty trainers, an old jumper and no make-up, bags under my eyes from lack of sleep, my hair in a mess – a way of saying to him in advance, 'Is this what you wanted to see? It wasn't worth putting yourself out.'

There was always this relentless determination to put myself down, this unhealthy self-disgust when the guy was charming and I had no reason not to meet him. My love life has been ruined by this destructive attitude.

I thought to myself, 'He'll clear off, or he'll do something inexcusable, come out with something that will allow me to slap his face and escape unscathed.'

I was incapable of looking a man straight in the face without feeling threatened. Unfortunately, he behaved impeccably. I couldn't find fault with anything, and he didn't make the slightest slip-up. The conversation revolved around work, until the moment he dared to say, 'If you get married, how will you manage? There aren't many men who would put up with their wife working nights.'

'Would you put up with it?'

'No. I wouldn't like to be all on my own in the evenings. It would be the same for the woman, who'd be on her own throughout the day. That tends to end in divorce.'

'Anyway, I'm fine as I am. I don't need a husband.'

Gradually, I found myself chatting to him. I liked the way he thought about women. As far as he was concerned, it was important to respect women, because the world would turn out badly without them.

He was the first boy who'd talked to me like that. When we had to say goodbye, I watched him intently again, thinking, 'If he tries something on, I'll read him the riot act.' But he didn't try anything at all. He just said, 'See you again very *very* soon, I hope?' With the emphasis on the 'very'.

After about ten dates he was still well behaved, still on time, still open-minded, friendly and handsome. We spent our brief romance strolling through parks. It was lovely – a well-behaved, peaceful little romance. We'd meet in front of my friend Souria's block of flats, and in the evening I managed to work things so that I could see him for a while or even have dinner with him. He was already looking further ahead. 'Just think. Picture us in the not-too-distant future, in my car with our two children, driving to Morocco for a holiday.'

I couldn't imagine myself in the future. The idea of having a husband and children scared me half to death. 'Hang on; hold your horses, do you already see me with kids? If that's the case, things will never work out between us.'

'Why are you always so negative?'

My heart beat more quickly when I was with him and there was always the risk of giving in to temptation and doing something stupid, so I was tough on him. Only once did he almost miss a meeting. He said, 'I can't meet you; my mother needs me.'

I threw a huge tantrum. I wanted to push him to the limit, be absolutely sure of his feelings for me – and to dominate him too.

'Listen, it's simple; I can't stay at Souria's for much longer; her parents are going to show up and wonder what I'm doing here! So, if you're not outside her flats at the time we arranged, you can find someone else. It's over.'

And I hung up.

Souria stood there, open-mouthed. She thought I was being stupid. I was behaving like a spoilt teenager and inwardly I felt dreadful, even if I told Souria that I couldn't care less whether he came or not. I was treating love like trench warfare and it was a war I had to win. However, I was no longer making fun of things like a clown who doesn't give a damn about his own misery. That evening I kept watch anxiously by the large window overlooking the car park where we were to meet. I was praying to myself, 'Please, Lord, let him come, that will shut me up.'

A car hooted and my heart began to thump. Souria said, 'Go on!'

'No, it can't be him! He's not going to drive over 30 miles and leave his mother high and dry just to come and see me!'

But it was him, so I raced for the door, while Souria shouted, 'Idiot! You're obviously in love!'

I refused to be in love; I wanted to maintain the impression of playing a game, of having won a battle over men in general by forcing this particular man to obey me.

I realised later to what extent romances between Arab girls and boys are damaged by the continual need for lying. Meetings kept secret from parents, schemes that only work with the collusion of male or female friends, of a cousin who's in the know but won't say anything because the girl is not his sister. Arab neighbourhoods are being remade in the image of an Arab village of the past, where relationships are wreathed in mystery and people skirt around things left unsaid. All this results in a complete lack of honesty about yourself. Who am I? What am I looking for? What is my real identity? I belong to a father who doesn't love me, so how am I going to learn how to love someone in my turn and, most importantly, how am I going to admit it to myself? In a society that outlaws the instinct of love, how do you control that instinct without drowning yourself in a sea of frustration?

Some of my French friends understand this because they grew up with us, but others think we're living on another planet and that we refuse to change. Going into town one afternoon or to the library is no big deal, is it? Nor is meeting your boyfriend in public. It's possible for them but it's forbidden for us. They have a little insight into the hassle we face in that they see some of the examples at close quarters, but they know nothing about what goes on indoors, what actually happens in our homes.

The others, the girls who live in the countryside in detached houses that we regard as the height of luxury in comparison to our council flats, don't understand at all. They think all these taboos are pathetic – and if they do try to understand, we're the ones who put them in their place. 'OK, drop it, you can't possibly understand.'

It's because we're ashamed of living like this. We're always ashamed, even with our best friends. We feel ashamed about everything: about our situations, about hiding our bodies, about our love lives. While other girls don't make a song and dance about their virginity, we feel deeply guilty about the most innocent of kisses. The smallest gesture of affection from a man is interpreted as an insult to our obligatory sense of propriety.

That evening I was not a French girl in love. Kader had come and I had triumphed over him. I was a proud Arab girl. If I'd listened to my heart, it would have said something quite different. When I went home that evening I was still a virgin. I knew that I wouldn't give way to temptation.

The next day, I didn't hear from Souria. Usually, the day after a date she'd always call me to hear the details. I decided to call her at her mother's flat.

'She isn't here at the moment.'

It was 3 p.m. on a Sunday afternoon and she wasn't there? She hadn't dropped by to see me and she hadn't called: it was odd. She still wasn't there in the early evening, but I didn't press her mother any further. You must never abandon so-called etiquette, which involves asking after the whole family and paying your respects to every single generation before having any chance of finding out some real information. Something serious had happened and if I pushed her mother too far, we'd be forbidden to see each other again. That evening, however, I was really worried so I called back.

'No, Leila, she isn't here. Actually, she's gone to visit her sister.'

That proved something was wrong. Souria didn't get on with her sister, who was too strict and uncompromising. They always send girls away when something serious has happened, and unsurprisingly it's always somewhere strict. Her mother's tone of voice clearly suggested I shouldn't call again. Three days later I made another attempt: still no Souria and no explanations, naturally. I tried to get in touch with her boyfriend but, as there was no answer, I decided to wait for him in the hallway of his block of flats.

He rushed over to me, and said, 'Leila, have you heard from Souria?'

'No, that's why I'm here!'

'You don't know what happened last Saturday then? But you were with her last Saturday, weren't you?'

'Yes, but earlier in the evening and then I left. Why, what happened?'

'We were both very stupid.'

I immediately thought that she'd slept with him and that her parents had found out. But it wasn't even that!

'You'd just left, I was passing in front of the building and, as she was all on her own, she told me to come up for five minutes. But the five minutes went by very quickly and her brother turned up.'

'She asked you to come up? Or did you insist?'

'No. It was her idea! She suggested I come up!'

'And you stayed with her in her parents' flat, all on your own, just the two of you?'

'For five minutes. We didn't do anything wrong! When her brother turned up, I hid behind the door in the back bedroom, but Souria was in such a panic that he suspected something. He found me and we had a fight. I tried to explain that I wanted to marry his sister, but he kicked me out! And I don't know where she is!'

This is what disgrace is. The fact that he had popped in for five minutes to visit his fiancée when the family wasn't at home and that he had been caught alone with her. My friend had taken an enormous risk. Even I wouldn't have done that. A girl doesn't decide on her own to open the door to a member of the male sex. Only her father or brother has the right to accept a visit by a stranger to the family.

Souria resurfaced after a fortnight, having lost a great deal of weight. Her father had tied her to her bed for five days, lying flat on her stomach with her hands and feet tied to the bedposts. They fed her like a dog – she couldn't move or turn over, and had to eat crouching down, so she had eaten virtu- ally nothing. If she asked to go to the toilet, her mother insulted her, saying, 'Why don't you wet yourself, it'll do you good.'

Her parents are from a region in Morocco where they've been known to slit a daughter's throat in the name of honour. Naturally, they forbade her boyfriend to see her or even look at her. Marriage was out of the question. Not only had they both failed to safeguard family honour, but there was also an aggravating circumstance: Souria's suitor was a Kabyle from Algeria. Souria's mother also had her reasons for rejecting him, completely ridiculous reasons that unfortunately counted. Souria's boyfriend's sister had married and Souria's mother had baked the cakes for her wedding, since the two mothers knew each other. Her refusal now arose from the fact that this family had supposedly made a fool of her.

'They approached me to make the cakes, didn't they? It was just so that their son could meet my daughter! And everyone knew about it except me!'

It just so happened that this wasn't even the case. Souria had fallen in love the first time she had seen this boy. His family had no idea about their relationship and they really loved each other.

Another more important cause for disgrace: Souria had brazenly invited a boy into her parents' flat, which brought her virginity into question. A girl capable of doing that is committing a serious sin. Bringing a man into the house isn't 'halal', but 'halam', 'halal' being what is allowed by God and 'halam' being a sin. So, Souria was a sinful daughter.

After she regained her freedom, Souria 'ate her mother's brain'. Translated from neighbourhood jargon, this expression was tantamount to saying that she finally succeeded in convincing her mother to forgive her by working like me in the meantime and giving her all her pay. The scandal subsided.

Souria was extremely careful after that, because her brothers were continually on her back. One of them was really crazy; even I was afraid of him, because if he caught me in the process of doing something 'halam', smoking or chatting to a strange man, he'd forbid Souria to see me. He never caught me out, but to safeguard my friendship with Souria I had to double the number of people against whom I had to be on my guard. If I saw her brother when I was going into the tobacconists, I'd immediately come out with a three-franc stamp.

The fact that it was impossible to communicate directly with a boy, even at the age of 20, led to my break-up with Kader. One day, he'd asked me to call him at home at a specific time.

'OK, but you'd better be there. I don't want someone else to pick up the phone.'

Unfortunately his sister answered, or a woman anyway. I panicked and immediately hung up the phone, furious at almost getting caught out because of him. Then I called back all the same. Politely and in Arabic, I said, 'Hello. Sorry to bother you, but may I speak to Kader?'

'May I know who wants to talk to my brother?'

'Er, I'm just a work colleague. I had something to ask him about work. Isn't he there?'

At that moment I heard his mother's voice in the distance, saying, 'Who's that tart who wants to talk to Kader? Who's that tart hanging around my son?'

She seized the telephone and screamed, 'Do you actually think my son's going to marry you?'

I hung up the phone after a barrage of insults. She didn't know me and I couldn't introduce myself to her, as I was a stranger. I was just a woman's voice asking to speak to her son, so it was only natural that she should gratuitously call me a tart. A girl doesn't phone a boy, that's 'halam'.

I stayed in the phone box, beside myself with anger. His sister didn't know me, but spoke to me as if she were talking to a dog. Her mother knew nothing about me and called me a tart. And this boy said he loved me and wanted to marry me? And give me children? And take me to Morocco on holiday?

That was it for me. Two families who live 30 miles from each other and who don't know each other? No point in trying to get past the obstacle: we'd never manage to persuade them to agree to a marriage. I didn't come from his region either. His mother had already labelled me, and my father wouldn't let me live 30 miles away, love or not . . .

I thought he might telephone, but I didn't answer, letting my father do it. I knew that as soon as Kader heard his voice he'd hang up. He didn't give up. The phone rang every ten minutes and my father got fed up with it. He gave me a funny look. 'These telephone calls are starting to annoy me. Perhaps someone is trying to contact you and is hanging up because I'm the one who answers?'

'No way! Apart from Souria, I don't know anyone who might be trying to call me. Maybe it's some girl calling one of my brothers! Why me?'

I surreptitiously took the phone off the hook. I didn't sleep all night.

When the telephone rang the next day, my father had gone and I said to my mother, 'Leave it, it must be Souria.'

I shut myself in the dining room.

'What's the matter with you? I've been trying to get hold of you since yesterday.'

'It's over. Leave me alone, sod off, I don't want to see you again.'

'You can't do that to me! I wasn't the one who insulted you, it was my mother, and I don't give a damn about my mother and sisters! Ignore them, they don't matter; it's just because I'm the only boy and they're trying to protect me! I had a go at my mother; I told her she didn't have any right to speak to you like that, that you're a girl from a very good family! My mother has lived her life. My sisters can live theirs, if they want. I'll live my life the way I want and with the girl I want!'

'Kader, nothing has been put in the tajine to cook and the tajine is already burning. If we were to get married, I'm the one who'd get torn to pieces.'

He had five sisters and a mother on his back: five potential sisters-in-law and a shrewish, possessive mother-in-law. It would never work; it would be better to call a halt to things before I fell deeper and deeper in love with him and finally ended up being rejected by his whole family.

'It's you I want to spend my life with! Forget my family!'

'It's better if you forget me, Kader . . . Leave me alone.'

He continued to try to contact me until the summer, when my parents were away in Morocco. He wanted us to spend a weekend together to sort things out. I refused. A weekend just with him, even miles from home, was much too risky: I might have given in to temptation. But it was hard, so hard. I was sad and now and then said to myself, 'Leila, you're a coward . . . You should've talked to your parents about it; you should've told them he was the love of your life. You should've forced them to listen, you should've fought for him, he seemed so sincere!'

Once, only once, I tried to talk to my mother about him,

and she'd replied, 'He's from that region, is he? That's not good, my girl!'

Neither he nor I could choose, unless we were prepared to break up two families at the same time and live completely alone, something that most of us don't dare to do.

My romance only lasted a few months, the year when I was 20. My heart didn't race for anyone after that.

August arrived. My parents went on holiday and I went back to being single and a loner. Because I'd rejected what I thought was impossible, I, the fly, now found myself trapped in the worst spider's web possible.

CHAPTER FIVE

A husband?

My family had returned from their holiday and the suitors who'd apparently been flocking to the door of our family's house in Morocco weren't mentioned again. Actually, the 'business' had already been sorted out in advance. My mother simply told me we were expecting a guest. All my father added was that we had to entertain him properly.

I continued to live my life and go out to work without attaching a great deal of importance to all this talk of a guest, and by early autumn I still hadn't been put in the picture.

He turned up one Sunday evening. It was during this period that the 'fiancée' of one of my brothers had been thrown out of her parents' house for having a relationship with a Muslim. My father had taken her in without a fuss; I didn't dare imagine his reaction if I'd asked the same thing. Unthinkable! A boy can have a relationship with a non-Muslim, but a girl can't.

Anyway, Melissa had decided to convert; she was submissive, obeyed the family's rules and had been on holiday with them to Morocco. For the first time in my life, I had a female friend in the house. She slept with me out of respect for decorum because she wasn't yet married to my brother. Melissa had been adopted by all of us, me in particular. It was a laugh sharing chores with her.

One day in the late autumn, the telephone rang and a man's voice asked to speak to my father.

'Papa, it's for you. Someone called Moussa.'

My mother seemed unusually fidgety.

'Moussa? Moussa? You're sure he said Moussa? That's the person who's coming over from Morocco.'

This Moussa was phoning to say that he'd be arriving by train that evening and my mother immediately wanted me in the kitchen to start cooking for this guest, who was apparently someone very important.

'Moussa is the boy who came to ask for your hand in marriage this summer.'

'Really.'

Although I might have looked unconcerned, I was actually totally freaked out. Until now any marriage requests mentioned in front of me had been irrelevant. I had either been too young or my parents hadn't thought he was good enough for me, so I hadn't paid them any attention. This time something told me that the trap was more dangerous than usual. I went to bed as if nothing was wrong, trembling and eaten up with anxiety.

Why was he making this trip? Had my parents come to some arrangement with him without telling me? Was he coming to look me over properly, to check the quality of the merchandise? If that were the case, I'd do my best to put him off. I was already in bed when my mother shouted, 'Leila! Come and help me! We have to welcome him properly.'

'No, I'm not helping.'

'Come and help me this minute, Leila! I'm telling you to come and help!'

'No! I'm tired. I'm working tomorrow, so no way.'

My mother did the necessary on her own, grumbling to herself. She didn't want to annoy my father before the stranger arrived. A good wife shouldn't annoy her husband about some little problem in the kitchen; it just isn't done. So she prepared a feast fit for a king on her own. I grew increasingly anxious as the cooking smells reached my nostrils, while bragging to Melissa, 'I don't bloody care! I'm going to sleep!'

My father drove to the station to pick him up around midnight and my mother came and shook me awake. 'Get up! Get up! You have to dress and do your hair. You have to greet him!'

I turned over very slowly in bed, still seemingly unconcerned. 'I'm sorry, but no way! He doesn't need to see me and I don't need to see him! Leave me alone!'

This time she began shouting. 'You will get up! And get a move on! Your father will soon be back with him! I'm warning you, Leila, you'll get a good thrashing if you're not dressed by the time he gets here!'

I'd never seen my mother so stressed. In her hurry to get herself dressed, she even forgot to yank my hair. I shouted 'No!' once more at her departing back. Melissa took it on herself to interfere in the kindest possible way.

'Leila, why don't you just make an effort? You meet him, everyone calms down and then you simply say, "No, I don't want to marry him."'

'You don't understand! You don't know them. If I agree to meet him, then the damage is done!'

'Don't be silly. What on earth are you talking about!'

'I just know! If he meets me and wants me, then I'm done for.'

Melissa is French, even if she'd decided to ignore the fact by marrying my brother. In her family no one would have been forced to marry a stranger. Of course, her father had told her to choose: my brother or her family. She'd chosen my brother and landed up with us. At least she'd had a choice.

I wouldn't have had that luxury. My father would rather have shut me away. I know how these things work for a girl like me. I was 20, I'd run away twice, I was rebellious, I liked going out, I smoked cigarettes, I worked nights, I'd tried to commit suicide, I wasn't my parents' idea of a dream daughter. They wouldn't risk my suitor changing his mind. They wanted me married off before I took it into my head to throw caution and my virginity to the wind.

While I wretchedly hugged my pillow and endeavoured not to give in, my mother welcomed the newcomer in the usual manner, greeting him three times over.

'Welcome, come in, you must treat our home as your own . . . '

I wailed over and over to myself, 'If you show your face, Leila, you're done for.'

I had absolutely no confidence in my ability to refuse. I knew very well that if I showed my face, my parents and my suitor would take this formal appearance as a de facto acceptance and then it would be a real hassle to turn the clock back.

'Leila, go and make some tea!'

I was seething with helpless rage. 'Make some tea and take it to him on a silver platter.' I saw the symbolic image of the submissive, well-bred young girl, ready to serve the first moron brought before her, because the family has made a decision.

I've spent my whole life serving men, but this time it felt as if I were selling myself to a man I didn't even want to know. My feelings of foreboding were becoming a reality. My childhood and teenage years were rising to the surface again like nausea. I was born to suffer; it would never stop; it was impossible to have some peace, to live my life without them worrying about my shitty virginity. I had no intention of selling it on the cheap. I felt like shouting, 'Here it is! If I could, I'd put a red light down there! It'll change to green when I decide! For the time being, I don't want anything to do with anyone!'

How could I make them see? How could I tell them, 'Don't worry, my hymen's still intact and that's the way it's going to stay! Don't you realise that I've been totally hung up since I was a little girl? That the last thing I want to do is get laid? Especially not by a stranger! Leave me alone; give me time to dream, to love, to choose!'

My parents were impervious to this type of argument. The culmination of a girl's education is marriage. The parents' role is to guide her towards marriage. Once married, she becomes her husband's responsibility. The father is relieved of his duty; he has done his job.

I hadn't even been able to buy my freedom with cash. I'd thought I could use my wages as some kind of protection against marriage, but that had been completely unsuccessful.

Melissa tried to cheer me up, saying, 'Come on, it's not so bad.'

More than anything, she was afraid that my father would slap me in front of everyone. I eventually gave in to my mother but, before throwing myself into the lion's mouth, I wanted see what 'he' was like.

'Melissa, do me a favour. Go into the lounge and see what he looks like.'

'And what excuse do you want me to make?'

'Then go and fetch something drying on the balcony – anything will do – and take a look through the window.'

'Are you crazy? Have you seen the weather? Your mother will ask what I'm doing out there!'

'Pretty please!'

Just our luck. The windows were steamed up, and she couldn't see a thing apart from my mother's back. She came back giggling. 'She's standing right in front of him. Nothing doing! Listen to me, stop being a pain. Go in there, take a look at him, he'll take a look at you, and then you can make up your mind, and say no!'

I decided to make the tea, as etiquette demanded, and take it into the lounge with me. I took malicious pleasure in adding three times more black leaf tea than mint and not enough sugar, to make it as bitter as possible. I congratulated myself on this shrewd move. He'd think that I didn't even know how to make tea. That should count as a black mark against me.

My mother had forced me to wear a *gandura*. She wanted me to do my hair and put on make-up, but I'd refused, and I'd left my messy hair tied back.

Melissa giggled at me, saying, 'This tea is really disgusting.'

I don't know why, but before walking into the lounge with my tray, glasses, teapot and cakes, I went over to examine his shoes. Like all visitors, he'd left them in the hall. Then and there, the decision I'd taken in advance became a gigantic *No* in my mind. *Never*!

Small, nerdy lace-ups, made of black leather, with a sort of mesh and little imitation holes on the upper. They were hideous. My father, who was much older than him, had good taste compared with those things. My suitor had no sense of style at all. I immediately realised what kind of guy they wanted me to marry. I dashed back into the kitchen right away, still carrying my tray of terrible tea.

'No way, Melissa! Have you seen his shoes?'

'That's so silly! You went to look at his footwear?'

She laughed until she cried, but I couldn't see anything funny about it.

'He's not the guy for me. That's obvious.'

'But how can you tell? You haven't seen him yet! You've only seen his shoes!'

'Those dorky lace-ups say it all. I bet he has a face to match!'

'It doesn't cost anything to go and have a look! Calm down; don't base your first impression on his shoes, that's stupid!'

'I don't like his shoes, so I won't like him!'

I was stubborn. I'd been shocked by those wretched shoes. This guy was a peasant. Those dusty, old-fashioned, shapeless, crappy lace-ups gave him away.

'Melissa, they've picked a North African peasant from the back of beyond! It's the little details that make shoes like that so awful. How can they want to fob me off with a guy who traipses around in those?'

I already felt humiliated at having to put up with this outdated performance and now it was even worse – I was being sold short. Even if I'd seen designer shoes, Dior-style shoes, I would have felt as if they were selling me like a whore to some guy who was rolling in it. If I'd seen trainers, I'd have labelled the bloke an unemployed dropout ready to nick all my money so that he could hang around in cafés. I wouldn't have been happy with any style of man's shoe; I didn't want to marry anyone. My dream man, the man I might love one day, didn't wear shoes. They were as unreal as he was.

I could picture this man from those shoes – this stranger who had infiltrated my home like a cuckoo. He was the nightmare I'd dreaded and those nerdy lace-ups confirmed it. Moreover, my parents had welcomed that dreadful pair of shoes with all the usual bowing and scraping so that they could ruin my life once and for all.

I could feel the vortex waiting to suck me down, weeks and bloody weeks of hassle, stress and battles to say 'no'. They weren't going to drop this matter in a hurry. The moment I was sucked into this vortex, I'd be done for. I'd want to say 'no' and 'no' again . . . and I wouldn't be able to.

I took in the tray. I should have tipped the teapot over him when he looked at me, but I didn't even raise my eyes. I said 'hello' looking the other way, barely touched his hand, didn't smile and left the room as briskly as I'd come in. My mother cornered me in the kitchen in a rage.

'You've gone too far this time. You could have at least sat down.'

'Sat down where?'

'Did you at least look at him?'

'I didn't want to look at him. I don't want to see him! He saw me, didn't he? Isn't that what you wanted? End of story. I don't want to see him.'

And I didn't actually see him that evening. Ordinarily, this would be humiliating for an Arab man. I wanted to annoy him; to make my feelings clear to him without saying a word, to make him sod off.

But he didn't sod off. The full extent of the disaster assumed frightening proportions. He'd come from Morocco specially, so everything had been pre-arranged.

I cried in the bedroom with Melissa; she was the only one who could understand.

'To hell with it! I don't want to get married. I don't want to get married.'

'Don't worry, Leila. Your parents have realised you don't want to, so they won't make you.'

'You haven't understood anything, have you? You're French, you're so naive. You were able to choose my brother and turn your back on your family, but I could never leave my family. Where would I go?'

She tried to make a joke of it, to tease me, saying, 'Did you even look at his face?'

'No. I couldn't give a damn about his face! I saw what he looked like from his shoes!'

I became obsessed with those shoes. Every time I mentioned them the others laughed, like Melissa. 'Cinderella wants to find the shoes that fit the prince!' I was only able to laugh about it myself after I'd woken up from my five-year nightmare.

When I was alone that night, tossing and turning in my bed, I talked to myself like a mad woman. 'It's unbelievable, I don't believe it, I don't believe it, I don't believe it.' Then I prayed. I asked God for help, but I didn't even get his answering machine. He was out and hadn't left a message.

The next day I felt calmer when I climbed out of bed. Knowing he was bound to stay for some time, I'd decided to lock myself in rather than risk bumping into him. I sent Melissa on a recce before coming out.

'Go and check he's not in the corridor.'

I successfully managed to avoid him like this for a fortnight in my own home. Melissa gave me a hard time about it.

'Go and talk to him yourself! Tell him you refuse once and for all! Look him in the eye and tell him straight out: I don't want to marry you, so get lost!'

Why not? Why couldn't I confront the bloke? I couldn't run away from him for ever. I probably secretly hoped that my parents would abandon the idea; that they loved me enough to understand how I felt. Really, it was their fault he had come here, so it was up to them to send him packing. I lived in hope . . . like a coward, I kept hoping.

I used work as an excuse, although my temp work had dried up at that time. I took a course of driving lessons to pass my driving test, just to avoid him the rest of the time.

After a fortnight my mother came to have a serious talk with me, acting as a go-between.

'Your father is starting to lose his temper. You must go and see Moussa. He's not a dog. You have to treat him as someone important and you have to come to an agreement with him.'

'Come to an agreement about what? Why?'

'Leila, this will turn out badly with your father!'

My brothers weren't much help either.

'You don't have any choice! You can't leave a guy hanging on until your ladyship deigns to speak to him! It's just not done!'

To top it all, my father said to me in Arabic, a clear sign that he was serious, 'Listen to me, my girl. Let me spell things out for you. Moussa has been here for two weeks. You've avoided him for two weeks, and he's been waiting patiently for two weeks. Now, you'll do me a favour; you'll go into the lounge, sit down beside him and come to an agreement with him.'

I'd run out of choices that day. I couldn't even make myself scarce, because my father wouldn't have let me leave the house. I could no longer imagine running away, I had no job, there was nowhere I could go, and even if I'd tried to run away, they were watching me so closely that they would have caught me this time. I knew they spied on everything I did. Big Brother was watching me 24 hours a day. So I did my best to look like a stupid slut no one would want to marry. I kept my eyes lowered or averted, as if he weren't in the room.

I gazed at my mother's houseplants. I didn't say a word for ten minutes, a quarter of an hour.

'So, how are things, Leila?'

'. . . / . . .'

'Do you know why I'm here?'

'. . . / . . .'

'At least look at me! Look at me!'

A feeling of rage, hatred and disgust swept over me; I felt an uncontrollable urge to insult him, to tell him, 'Go away, clear off, I want you out of my life, I don't want to look at you, get the hell out of here!'

However, if I did that I was dead. My father would give me a thrashing that was bound to be far worse than anything I'd ever had in my life. The script had already been written: beating, house arrest, beating; he would have forced me to surrender, if I didn't commit suicide first. When my father lost his temper, I never knew how far he might go and I was petrified that I might not survive. This was the final battle between him and me; he was armed with the weapon of authority, which he couldn't lay down, and I was defenceless. My only hope was that I could put this suitor off once and for all and that he would give up. Even then I wouldn't escape a beating. I would have shamed the family, trampled my father's honour underfoot.

My mother had followed me into the lounge. I was forced to look at him, since she was there as an observer to see how I was acting with him. She sat down as though there was nothing wrong, her tone urbane, airy, as if to say, 'Go on, talk to him, let him hear what your voice sounds like.'

'So, Leila, what are you chatting about?'

As if this guy and I were best mates!

'Nothing special.'

He was sitting down, leaning forward slightly. I noticed he was a little tubby and taller than me. He looked every bit his age: 35. I thought he was awful and, more than anything, stupid to want to marry a girl he'd never seen before and to persevere, even when everything about my behaviour told him I wasn't interested.

Ordinarily, his pride would have been wounded. If I'd behaved like this with a local boy, he would have reacted aggressively. With this guy I felt as if I were banging my head against a brick wall.

I thought about it a lot later. On the one hand, the bloke was just following 'tradition'. Even if a girl appeared reluctant, she didn't count; it was only her father who counted. But, most importantly, he wanted to be married in France so that he could acquire French nationality.

He was tall, mature, square-shouldered and not actually as ugly as all that. Old-fashioned, certainly, but he'd come from North Africa: he had mitigating circumstances. He couldn't even force me to accept him: my father was the only one who could do that. He was only here by my father's consent; he wanted to marry me with my father's blessing. I shouldn't even have held it against him personally. The guy had just done what hundreds of other guys do on a regular basis. He'd simply introduced himself to the family in Morocco, offering to marry a 'Moroccan girl from France'.

It's awful not being able to talk normally to someone, to say, 'Listen. Please don't do this to me. I know it's the custom. I know that this is the way girls are married off, but not me. Don't be unkind!' You can't talk to the suitor chosen by your father like that. You'll find yourself repeatedly slammed up against a wall until you give in.

When I think about it now, I could kick myself. I say to myself, 'Leila, you're such a coward! At that moment, in the lounge, you should have said "no", even if it meant a beating. You could have jumped out of the window and run away. You could've found a job since you've always worked. You could perhaps have salvaged at least the dream of being free to marry a man you could have loved, instead of being humiliated, regarded as an insignificant object and delivered by your father into the hands of a stranger.' What my father wanted me to submit to was nothing short of rape.

I hated everyone at that time. I hated that custom. Why had I been born a girl? Why hadn't I been born a boy? I wanted to be an Arab woman, to have respect for God and religion, but the way a man did. If I'd been a man, I'd have been able to live a life that was worlds apart from this nightmare, and I'd never have forced a woman to marry me.

I could feel the spider's web woven tightly around me. Moreover, there wasn't just one spider waiting to devour me; there was an entire clan – my family, my cousins, my neighbourhood, my community – they were all lying in wait for little flies like me. They were going to paralyse me, wind their threads around me, and turn me into a mummy for that guy to devour at his leisure on our wedding night.

It was too hard to make the decision to take to my heels, wrench open the door and say to myself that I was leaving everything, my family, my identity papers, my life. Where would I have gone? To the cops? This wasn't any of their business. To my knowledge there wasn't a single family in the neighbourhood who would have had the guts to take me in. There wasn't a social worker who'd have taken me under her wing. This was a domestic matter; no one cared a damn about it.

I was French and an adult. If I allowed myself to be trapped into this forced marriage that was my fault. No one had actually spelled that out to me yet, but I had the feeling that this was the case. If this guy wanted me, it was so that he could live in France with valid identity papers – and why shouldn't this practice have become natural, customary, and even traditional after a while? He'd said to my parents that he would live wherever I wanted – in Spain, Italy or France – a hypocritical gambit to make them think that he wasn't marrying me just to acquire French nationality. It was also a way of signalling to them: 'I won't repudiate her.' As far as my father was concerned, nothing could be worse than a repudiated daughter. Better that she should be an old maid.

Some men marry, consummate the marriage and then, once they've obtained their papers, they do a runner. I didn't have the impression that he would do that so readily – and anyway the harm would have been done, as far as I was concerned.

I was filled with hatred for him. I hated myself, my parents. It was the end of my life as a young Western woman. I was being reclaimed by a tradition that merely presented men with new opportunities: a wife = identity papers = social security = income support.

You spend your whole childhood trying to escape the time-honoured tradition of family-arranged marriages, you listen to other people's stories as though they were legends from ancient times, but the reality is that you fall back into it – you're even kicked back into it, if necessary. This is because the deal has changed: there has been a return to conventionality. Intermarriage is now the order of the day; intermarriage between members of the same clan, if possible.

My father summoned me to the bedroom immediately after this meeting. He wasn't interested in any discussion, any compromise. 'It's him and no one else. You don't have a choice.'

I couldn't breathe. I was choking with despair.

My brothers took over. 'Leila, you must say yes. He's a nice guy; you couldn't find a better guy. You don't have a choice.'

The cousin who had acted as the go-between phoned from Morocco, and other cousins, some of whom I didn't even know, phoned from all over France. The telephone rang continually; everyone had the same message: 'This is a good marriage.'

Meanwhile my father, who knew me well, played on my sensitivity. Despite everything they've done to me, I love my family. I would have liked to be able to uproot myself, cut the umbilical cord, but I couldn't and I still can't today. Despite those feelings of hatred, which wasn't even hatred really, my father was still my father and my mother was still my mother. I was born like that. I was still young but, at the age of 20, I felt as if I were twice as old. Most 20-year-old girls have friends, go out, eat in restaurants, go to the cinema, flirt if they aren't yet married, study, travel and even fall in love, but I was different – after a frustrating adolescence, I had landed up in the spider's web.

My parents gave my future husband bed and board and did his laundry. He didn't touch a penny of his savings; he had an easy time of it, just waiting to obtain his papers in France and everything else.

Prompted by helpless rage, I changed tactics. The girl who didn't use make-up started to wear it caked on her face like a tart – a desperate counter-attack with outrageous lipstick, tons of black kohl, enough mascara to stick my eyelids together and a triple layer of foundation. I used everything I'd teased my friend Souria about for my new look, including skimpy, figure-hugging tops, loose, blow-dried hair and three earrings.

I was just digging myself in deeper, though, because he was finding me increasingly attractive. He didn't even think I looked tarty. Even cigarette smoke didn't seem to put him off. I went down to the entrance hall of the flats to have a fag, I went back upstairs to give him a whiff, then went back down again to smoke another, and so on . . . nothing doing.

One day he suggested we go out to a restaurant, so that we could get to know each other better. I said, 'No thanks, I've got things to do.' He suggested going for a drink, going bowling, anywhere I wanted. 'No way! No thanks, I've got to go to work.'

I'd said to my father with tears in my eyes, 'Do what you think is best for me,' hoping he'd think it over. If he'd loved me he would have sent that bloke home. For a few seconds I'd thought he might . . . but he gripped me firmly by the shoulder. 'It's him and no one else, daughter. Don't worry, everything will work out.'

For once I really did what he wanted and I pleased him by giving up my life, my future. He had no idea how much he was ruining my life. He was positive he was acting for my own good, for my protection and to safeguard our honour; bloody honour.

That man made himself at home with my father's blessing until the end of October. One day I bumped into him in the town centre. I was with Souria. He invited us to have a drink in a café with one of my brothers. I refused to be seen with him and when Souria asked me who he was, I replied, 'A friend of my brother's. Nobody important.'

I was ashamed to tell my best friend the truth. Me, the big mouth who'd made such a fuss about declaring, 'Me? Never!' I was still hoping for some miracle; that he'd change his mind; that his train would be derailed . . . why not?

Melissa had taken the trouble to talk to him and was still trying to make me feel better. 'Leila, he's not a bad man; you might be happy with him.'

Eventually he left, because the plan was to sort out the Moroccan marriage certificate in the spring and return imme-diately to France for the 'paper marriage'. I wouldn't be the first woman from my neighbourhood to stand before the Mayor with red-rimmed eyes. No one is fooled, but it's a system that works.

Perhaps I'd be able to come up with a way out before then? All kinds of ideas ran through my mind in a bid to avoid the marriage. Find another guy, for example, and marry him first – but I was totally incapable of carrying out that kind of plan and bringing such shame on my father. What else? Give my virginity to the first man who came along, then confess to my family? Even less likely. If I did that I was sunk for the rest of my life. Even if I really fell in love, no one would want any-thing to do with me.

My mind wouldn't rest. Day and night this little fly strug-gled frantically to escape. Barely ten days had passed since he'd left before he called my father. 'I've been thinking. The earlier we sort out the Muslim marriage certificate the better. At least we won't have to worry and we'll be able to start the engagement.'

My father thought he was moving too fast, but he was just concerned about the financial side of things, and the other man was sparing no expense. 'I'll pay for the trip. I'll come to France and collect you, then take you back to Morocco with me. We'll sort out the Muslim marriage certificate and, that way, when people see me with her and think she's my wife, they'll be right, because she will be officially!'

I heard the conversations, because the telephone was in the hall. My father didn't even take the trouble to explain it to me in detail.

'Get ready to go to Morocco. We're leaving in a fortnight with your mother!'

'Why's that?'

'You're getting married.'

'Hang on a minute, Papa. Didn't he say it would be in the spring? What's the rush? And what about my brothers? They won't be there.'

'The quicker this is done, the better it will be for everyone. We can stop worrying then!'

I spent the whole time between that phone call and the moment I started my journey to Morocco in tears. Two weeks . . . how could I find a way out in two weeks? I'd really hit the jackpot with my behaviour. My future husband must have thought to himself, 'If I don't grab her quickly, she'll escape my clutches . . . '

He came back to France on the double and everyone climbed into the family van. He sat in the front next to my father; my mother was in the middle with one of my brothers. I sat on my own in the back, as far away from everyone as possible.

I slept through the journey across France and Spain. They couldn't get a word out of me and I didn't eat. I dreamed of an accident that would send us into the next world; at least there I wouldn't suffer any more. Or else I'd be the only survivor . . . or he'd be the only one killed. The families would mourn him and he'd never be mentioned again. A widow before I was even married. Slowly and silently I went out of my mind; I'd never been given anything I'd wanted in life. Not my father's love, or men's respect, or the Prince Charming for whom I'd been waiting and who'd whisk me off to live somewhere else, who'd share everything with me, allow my family to stay with us in the holidays, and the rest of the time . . . to just *live*.

I wanted God to take care of everything for me, to show me some kindness in sorting out my destiny, so that I could stop feeling guilty, trapped, unloved and tossed about on life's waves like some insignificant cork. God never put in an appearance, despite my prayers.

The mood seemed quite normal in the car, apart from my silence. My father got along very well with him. My mother was delighted, proud. They hadn't heard a peep out of me and they didn't care. When we boarded the boat at Algesiras, 'Monsieur Moussa' thought everything was going well, that we were celebrating, that he would be able to kiss me, that we'd act like two people madly in love. He asked me several times with an infatuated look in his eye if I wanted to take a stroll on deck with him.

'No! We're not married yet!'

This answer, which brooked no argument and which was in accordance with hard-line tradition, really meant 'Don't come near me, don't touch me! What little time I have left is mine and mine alone.'

I didn't even allow him to sit beside me on deck, when there was a seat free. Faster than a snake I snatched up my little brother and literally threw him into the seat on my right. 'Someone's sitting there. It's taken. My brother's sitting there!'

This hopeless battle was childish and desperate. One day or another I would have to allow this stranger to touch me, kiss me, take me to his bed. I refused to think about it. He physically repulsed me. He wasn't ugly and he wasn't stupid, because he'd understood my standpoint perfectly well and had never forgotten it; he was just a symbol of the system.

Some women have told me how they learned to love the husbands they were forced to marry. For me it was unthinkable. Too many restrictions over the years, too many taboos and attacks, had turned me into some kind of untouchable, unless it was with my permission and my love.

Going through customs is always strange. Taking two rugs through instead of the one that was 'authorised' meant slipping the official a few notes. It was a real production that I should have found funny, but that totally wound me up.

'Maman! Why did you have to buy rugs in France? Anyway, why two?'

'For the engagement! One for us, one for Moussa's family! That's tradition!'

'Then pay the man!'

'Absolutely no way! He was rude to me! It makes me sick; if anything should happen to me . . .'

'Stop it, Maman! And don't even think about clawing your own face either!'

I wanted to hit someone, even her, to make her realise what respect stopped me from screaming: 'There are much nicer rugs in Morocco. Why are you making our lives hell over a piece of shit bought at the market for 300 lousy francs? A manmade acrylic thing!'

But it was 'her' rug. In the end my father handed over the cash. He had no choice, otherwise we'd have been there for hours and we'd have lost the rug. However, he also discussed it endlessly, and the marriage, and the family, and this . . . and that . . . I wanted to beat his brains out to make him understand what respect still stopped me from saying: 'What's the point of throwing a fit when you know that in the end you'll stump up the cash! It's just another form of etiquette! They think we're rich because we've come from France.'

My mother had brought everything with her. The van was jam-packed: orange juice, fruit, sweets . . . and her daughter, who was just another parcel.

There was more etiquette to be observed when we arrived. The parents of the husband-to-be came to the house to officialise the request for my hand in marriage. My mother-in-law was a shrew. Even my mother looked askance at her. A multicoloured scarf, and tattoos on her forehead, nose and chin. The shifty expression of a vicious woman contemplating her world: in this case, me.

His father, wearing a djellaba, hat and white Turkish slippers, looked friendly. They were wealthy but simple people, and I discovered that my father-in-law was an extraordinarily kind, peace-loving man. My future brothers-in-law were also nice, and I couldn't find any fault with them. Moussa was the last member of his family to marry. His eldest brother, who'd only just tied the knot, was already in the process of obtaining a divorce, because his mother didn't like his wife. Not a good sign. She was the type of mother-in-law who hates all her daughters-in-law without exception. I soon discovered the family secrets about her. After being repudiated the first time, she was lucky enough to remarry this good man, because he was a cousin of the family and it was essential to restore their honour. She must have wanted to get her own back by ensuring that her sons repudiated their wives in their turn.

She examined me closely from head to toe. I felt as if the smallest detail of my face was being scrutinised by her tiny piercing eyes. My father was ill at ease with her. He didn't like her either; her spiteful nature showed in her face. My father-in-law was the complete opposite, though. He behaved perfectly and very respectfully. I liked the man immediately.

I said my hellos. Etiquette. Then I fled to the top floor of my aunt's house and they didn't see me again. In any case, in this type of negotiation no one spoke to the daughter before the papers were signed in front of the Aduls, Islamic notaries who are paid to record all administrative acts. They discussed money, jewellery, rugs, food, but not the bride.

Fortunately, we went to visit my maternal grandfather in the mountains, a break that did me the world of good, because I loved that man. I spent a day and night in Berber territory. It rained, the mountain was muddy, the car got stuck, and my mother twisted her ankle and lost a piece of jewellery. We had to stay longer than planned, when we were needed for the wedding preparations. If I'd been superstitious I would have said that none of the signs boded well.

I had a strange dream that night. In the dream a man stood before me. He was dressed all in white and had a long white beard and a turban. He said to me, 'Don't worry, Leila. I'll always be here to protect you, come what may.'

'You want to protect me, but it's too late.'

'Don't worry. Everything will be all right.'

The next morning the gold ring I'd been wearing on the ring finger of my left hand before going to sleep was now on my right hand. I must have taken it off in my sleep.

I left my grandfather's village feeling as if the past two days had been the last holiday of my life. I love that isolated Berber village in the mountains; I couldn't live there, since I'm too used to the luxury of electricity and running water, but I felt protected when I was with that proud, indomitable old man.

'Is he a good man, this man you're marrying?'

'He's from a good family, Grandfather.'

Again, respect prevented me from complaining. He couldn't help me. I was just his granddaughter and my father was the man with all the authority; he was the only person who could decide what happened in my life.

Once back in the town, there were more chores to do in connection with the wretched wedding. Moussa had to take me to buy the ring and other pieces of jewellery that the groom traditionally has to present to his fiancée. I was wrung out with grief; the people around me must have realised it, but everyone was acting as though nothing was wrong. Whenever I was with my father, I continued to reiterate my refusal, still hoping that the situation might come to a head one way or another.

'I don't want to go with Moussa. Let him deal with it on his own! I don't give a damn! I can't take any more.'

'How do you expect him to do that? You're the one who's going to be wearing those rings, after all!'

'I couldn't give a bloody damn! Do what you like. I couldn't care less!'

I was making the most of my aunt's protection; my father respected her too much to hit me in front of her. Also, and because of him, I was 'betrothed' to a man, so he no longer had the right to beat me for the time being and the other man didn't have the right to beat me yet . . .

'Leila! Get dressed. I'm going to take you to meet Moussa myself! You must go and buy the rings!'

'If it's the ring you're so worried about, here's one. This one suits me, so tell him to buy what he wants using this as an example. I don't bloody care.'

'You're going!'

Despite being betrothed I was in danger of being given a thrashing; he was annoyed and knew perfectly well that I couldn't care less what he was saying. My aunt discreetly made a sign to me to obey, but I categorically refused to go jewellery shopping on my own with Moussa.

'All my life you've been going on and on about not being alone with a man! I need a chaperone!'

I wanted to avoid all contact with him as much as possible until the very last minute.

'I don't want to hear another word! You're going!'

My father pushed me into the taxi beside my husband-to-be. I was pinned up against him, alone with him for the first time and so tense that I ached all over. He'd made considerable efforts to alter his image to impress me. He looked unrecognisable, elegant; he was even trailing an umbrella around with him, probably with some idea of looking like a gentleman.

I think he realised how much contempt I felt for him. Every time he'd try to move closer to me, I looked disgusted. He made the most of the nearness afforded by the taxi, which made me feel sick. Up until now there had always been a brother or uncle between him and me. Until she's married, a woman must not even be touched lightly by another man. In that taxi I was hemmed in, squeezed up tightly against him. If he'd made a single move, I would have slapped him, even though I knew what the outcome of this charade was and that there was no escape.

One of Moussa's sisters-in-law ended up accompanying us around the jewellery shops. She was a filthy rich middle-class woman who was used to ordering maids around and who gazed at me haughtily as if to say, 'Is this the woman who's going to be Moussa's wife?'

She might just as well have said, 'Is that it?' If only I'd been able to vent my feelings on her . . .

As the French-born daughter of a factory worker, I wasn't much of a catch as far as those people with their wealthy lifestyle were concerned. The woman was a teacher and her father was a university rector; they were 'caviar' intellectuals confronted by a local girl more accustomed to washing dishes than being served from a silver platter. However, it was through me that Moussa was going to get his hands on something much more precious than his family's silver platters – papers for France.

Impossible to eat, impossible to drink: the closer the time came, the more choked I felt. I had only been able to swallow a couple of mouthfuls of tea before we started looking round the jewellery shops. Our mission: to find a ring I liked but above all which met with my sister-in-law's approval. We're never really free to choose, in actual fact; nothing belongs to us. The gift always has to get the seal of approval from someone else. I soon realised that my sister-in-law was really there to ensure that I cost as little as possible. My husband-to-be might be rich, but he was also tight-fisted. Every time I saw something I liked, he said no. So I thought to myself, 'You want me, do you? Then you're going to cough up! Get your wallet ready.'

The jewellery shop told me the price and I pulled a face. 'Isn't there anything else? It doesn't matter if it's a little more expensive.'

Moussa waited in the background and my sister-in-law made a face at a ring costing 4,000 dirhams. 'No, it's old-fashioned; have that one instead.'

She was simply trying to save him 2,000 dirhams, but I stood up to them, so we left that jewellery shop, and in front of the next shop window, my sister-in-law made her choice. 'That one isn't bad. I'm going in to ask how much. Wait here for me!'

She came out looking determined, and saying, 'It's perfect!'

I stood there looking scornfully into the window, and said, 'I'm sorry, I don't like that at all.'

It was a real pleasure driving them both up the wall; I threw myself into the game, acting the prima donna. Let him pay through the nose; money was the sinew of this petty jewellery war between him and me. It was the only ground I could gain, because he was really stingy.

I was delighted with myself. I chose one of the most expensive rings, a solitaire, as my engagement ring, and a wedding ring with diamonds. Almost 6,000 dirhams – that's a lot in Morocco, much more expensive than the dowry.

It was hard for me to do any more. If only I'd been able to go to Cartier. He would probably have said to me, 'Go back to your mother!' There were also bracelets and earrings. I bought seven gold bracelets, the most expensive ones, and another really chunky one and various earrings. Oriental slippers and kaftans of all colours embroidered with gold thread. I felt that the more over the top I went, the more his wallet would suffer. I was supposed to pay for his wedding ring according to tradition. My cousins had told me that, but I deliberately hadn't brought any money with me.

Generally a good Muslim should not wear a gold wedding ring, but must make do with a discreet silver one. I chose the gold one costing 200 dirhams, instead of the silver one at 30 dirhams, and he had to pay for it himself, since I said, 'I'm so sorry, I didn't know.'

When I got back to my aunt's house, I left him standing

there without so much as a 'goodbye' or a 'thank you'. Horrible.

That night I couldn't sleep. I cried in my aunt's arms. She also cried.

'I don't want to get married.'

'If only I could help you.'

The next day I had a splitting headache. They made me go to the hairdresser and to the hammam. I went on my own, which was breaking all the rules. I wanted at least a little time to myself before the final scene that was going to unite me with this stranger.

After that I again took refuge in my aunt's house. I was safe there for a while. My mother was looking after the guests. I heard the whoops, my mother-in-law roaring with laughter; everyone was happy and thought it was strange that I should isolate myself like this and that I should be so miserable.

They categorised me as a modest young woman, a virgin upset at leaving her parents. It was more practical than asking questions about my anguish and my all too obvious refusal. I was the sheep being led to sacrifice on the day of the Aid El Kabir festival; after penning me up in a corner, they were going to unsheathe the knife and slit my throat.

Everything was done without me. There's nothing surprising about that. The fiancée is kept somewhere safe, like an untouchable treasure. She's only displayed to the public at the last moment. Moussa self-consciously came to stand next to me, my aunt left the room and he tried to steal a kiss.

'No. I'm sorry, but we're not married yet.'

'I don't understand you, but you'll get over it.'

He looked a little annoyed but he left and I cried again, in disgust. He thought he owned me after all those pieces of jewellery; he must have said to himself, 'I've paid for her, so now I can touch her!'

When my father came to see me, I begged him, kissing his hands, his forehead, his feet; I threw myself onto my knees. 'Papa, I'm begging you, I don't want to get married . . . Papa, I don't want to get married . . . Papa, I don't want to get married.'

I wept, prostrate at his feet like a slave before her master. This was the home stretch before the point of no return.

'Don't worry, daughter. Everything will be all right.'

He walked out of the room without the slightest display of emotion. He didn't love me. No one loved me. I thought again of Kader, who'd loved me and whom I'd rejected like an idiot for fear of landing myself with a cantankerous mother-in-law, for fear of braving my parents over the small problem of place of birth. The mother-in-law waiting downstairs for me was going to give me a really hard time, and so was her son.

Kader . . . I wouldn't be in this mess if Kader was downstairs; Kader was handsome, loving, attentive, and I would have been happy.

Left to my own devices, I waited for them to come and fetch me, late in the evening, fully dressed, my hair done, like a doll taken from her box. I felt completely depersonalised. I wasn't myself. I'd almost go as far as to say that the real Leila was dead. All that was left was a kind of ghost. My aunts and cousins whooped as I walked past. My young cousin was holding a large lighted candle. I lowered my eyes; I couldn't bring myself to look at the people around me.

Everyone was examining me, my kaftan, and the jewellery I was wearing – pieces my father had given me, because I was not yet wearing the jewellery given to me by my in-laws. The women were counting those gems; they were probably working out how much my father thought his daughter was worth.

My mother had pulled out all the stops for the occasion. Bracelets, rings – I didn't have enough fingers to wear them all. Henna on my hands and feet. Although I was decked out in all this finery, they had kept things to a minimum, because I'd refused the usual ceremonies. If I'd followed etiquette, there would have been music, singing and little girls dancing around me. You have to be happy to enjoy the lavish celebrations of a Moroccan wedding ceremony.

The Aduls had read from the Koran. They had already put the chair in the place where I was to sign the marriage register. I had nothing to say. All I had to do was sign a document in front of them: a wretched document before those judges who were authorised to draw up the marriage certificate, the only document valid in Morocco.

Everything had been written down in advance in Arabic: 'The daughter of Mr so-and-so declares that she is a spinster and a virgin and therefore becomes the property of the son of Mr so-and-so, in return for a dowry of . . .'

Eight hundred and fifty dirhams for me. A dirham is worth about one euro. I wasn't worth very much.

They then questioned the father.

'Do you agree to give your daughter to this man?'

'Do you agree to a dowry of 850 dirhams?'

'The husband states that the fiancée is a virgin to the best of his knowledge. Sign here!'

This is a statement about which men are never certain. If the woman isn't a virgin because she's been married before, this fact must be recorded as a defect: 'The woman is not a virgin.'

I think this detail is horrible.

The happy father signed, followed by his daughter. The mother never signs. Finally the husband signed. I was handed a wad of notes representing the dowry, which I would have liked to throw in Moussa's face.

When I think back to that scene, I always ask myself, 'Why, at that time, your last chance, didn't you jump up and say "To hell with the lot of you! I don't want anything to do with this man!"'

That question will haunt me for the rest of my life.

Moussa signed with a happy smile. My hands trembled when I had to sign in my turn. Then the photographer did his job. It was particularly important not to mess up that moment. I was devastated. One of my legs was shaking of its own volition; I couldn't control it any more. I felt empty inside. I'd never experienced such a feeling of emptiness before. My body was alive, but inside I was dead. During the compulsory photo session with all the members of the family, I was supposed to carry on playing the hypocrite and smile, but I couldn't raise a ghost of a smile. All the pictures are of a girl weeping.

The ceremony lasted until 4 a.m. I changed my clothes and put on one of the kaftans Moussa had given me, with gold-embroidered slippers. I had four little bridesmaids clustered around me. The women joked: 'Leila, you're going to give us nothing but little girls. You know what they say? They say that a future bride surrounded by little girls will give her husband little girls. Your mother produced nothing but boys; you'll produce nothing but girls!'

I was placed on a chair standing on a table covered with a white cloth, while he sat on another chair next to me: the king and queen of the day on their respective thrones.

He slipped the ring onto my finger, and I was given milk and dates, symbolising wealth and fertility.

That was the only time during this nightmare when I was able to give the faintest of mocking smiles: the husband usually delicately bites off a small piece of the date offered to him by his bride. That clown devoured the whole thing. I stifled a nervous giggle, because I felt ready to dissolve into tears.

This initial ceremony united me permanently to that man: I was done for; I was really married. Everything felt wrong and unreal, though – perhaps because I still had the right to reject him and keep my virginity until the other ceremony, the massive reception my parents would organise over the summer: a ceremony at the end of which a loveless wedding night was waiting.

CHAPTER SIX

Under a curse

I COULD'VE BEEN THE happiest of girls and young brides if I'd realised from birth that my father loved me.

From my teens I'd spent my life trying to make my father understand that he could trust me because, as we are believers, I'd been brought up to respect our religion. I probably went about it badly. 'Leave me in peace, let me be, I don't need someone spying on me all the time to find out how I'm tying my hair, who I'm speaking to and what underwear I've got on!'

Like Souria and so many other young girls, I was weighed down by the constant burden of being female. A woman's body is a congenital sin; a daughter only really exists in her father's eyes as a domestic servant kept locked in her room and a gift-wrapped parcel of virginity to be presented to the man of his choice. Fortunately, I wasn't one of those girls who are forced to wear headscarves or who choose to wear the headscarf for a little peace and quiet, but my life had always been a living hell. Moreover, I had struggled in vain for nothing: I was married.

I felt so ashamed that I didn't tell my best friend or anyone else about it and, on my return to France, I continued to act as if I were still single.

I was trapped fast by the marriage contract that had been signed before the Aduls. In Morocco you still needed the man's permission to divorce. The husband who repudiated his wife could throw her out without any income, stripped of social status and despised by others. Her own children were even sometimes taken away from her; she was the one who had to shoulder the 'disgrace' suffered by her family and her community. A new law passed in 2004 at the instigation of King Mohammed VI authorises divorce requested solely by the wife and guarantees to safeguard her rights, but this was not yet the case at the time of my marriage.

Even supposing I refused to see the husband they'd forced on me, which was theoretically possible (as long as I could persuade my father), Moussa could initiate proceedings in Morocco ordering me to return to the conjugal home. They'd search for me and one day, on my way to visit my family in Morocco for a holiday, I'd find myself held in customs, and then dragged before the magistrate. Moussa would be able to come and collect me, shut me away in his parents' house by force or repudiate me.

This is what I called the spider's web; I was stuck in a labyrinth, vainly seeking a way out.

Moussa regularly called home to put out feelers and play the husband.

'How are things?'

'Fine.'

'Do you need anything?'

'No.'

I certainly didn't need anything from him. He wrote me

love letters, in French, scattered with phrases like 'I love you' and 'I miss you terribly'. It was very good conventional French, rather laughable and formal. When a letter arrived, my father would solemnly hand it to me and my mother would insist, 'You must reply to Moussa! You can't not reply; it's not done! He'll be pleased to receive some news!'

I would write four lines by way of reply, a silly little note, folded in two. 'Everything's fine, the family say hello, ciao!'

I was perfectly happy while he was far away. I was working at the factory again and one day I screwed up enough courage to tell Souria that I was married. I had distanced myself a little from her to avoid doing so, but we'd always shared our misfortunes and our small pleasures and my family were now trying to put a wedge between us under the pretext that I was married. They were trying to run her down; her 'reputation' was no longer compatible with my new status.

'Maman, I'm going out.'

'Where are you going?'

'Just to get a breath of fresh air!'

'Don't be long and don't go anywhere!'

Such a nice phrase that! 'Don't be long going nowhere.'

I was programmed to obey, but I didn't even bother to let it get to me any more. Souria lived five minutes from my home in the neighbourhood.

'Leila! What's happened to you? Have you been ill?'

'No, just work . . . and run-ins with my parents . . . no changes there . . . '

'All the same, I haven't heard from you at all.'

'I'll explain; it's rather complicated.'

Before we could have a quiet private chat, I had to spend five minutes talking to her mother and sisters as etiquette demanded.

In whispers Souria told me about her boyfriend, whom she was still seeing secretly. I didn't say a word as she gave me a blow-by-blow account of her double life and, deep down, I envied her courage.

We were always careful to make sure that no one was listening behind the door of her room. Eavesdropping on what their daughters are telling each other is one of the favourite games played by parents.

Souria was fine. She was working, and had passed her driving test and bought a car. This was the height of freedom. I listened to her, thinking, 'That's it . . . I'm dead; it's all over for me! She's had a rough time, but she's pulled through and I haven't.'

'You're acting strangely, Leila; you're acting really strangely. What's up with you? Are you going to tell me what's wrong or what? You're different; even your expression is different! Normally, you chat, you have a laugh. This isn't the Leila I know.'

I didn't know where to begin to admit my defeat.

'I went to Morocco, you know.'

'Why didn't you tell me? And why did you go to Morocco in the winter?'

'Well . . . actually . . . I got married.'

'Wait, say that again, slowly . . . '

'Souria, I got married.'

'Are you taking the piss?'

'No, Souria, I'm married.'

I began to snivel with the shame of it. I'd just said 'I' got married as if I was the one who'd wanted to and not 'my parents married me off'. But she wasn't taken in.

'Where did you get this guy from? You never told me about him!'

I carried on lying.

'He's a guy I used to meet every summer. I went out with him for a time and bumped into him again this year and here we are . . . he asked me to marry him.'

'Yeah . . . but . . . well . . . you never talked about him.'

'It was just a summer thing . . . it's been going on for ages.'

She looked at me, frowning, trying to persuade herself that this really was love, but I hadn't uttered the magic words and tears welled in my eyes despite my best efforts.

'But . . . you are happy, all the same?'

'Of course I'm happy.'

It's terrible never being able to shake off this shame. Shame for being beaten, shame for being locked up, shame for being married. Shame for lying to happy people. *Shame* for not finding the courage and the way to say 'To hell with it', and walk out, slamming the door at the age of 20.

Souria pretended to believe me and didn't ask me any more about it.

When her mother saw the traces of henna on my hands and the ring on my finger, she made no bones about gloating over her daughter.

'Oh, congratulations, you're married, are you? I shall call your mother to congratulate her! Have you seen that, Souria? Have you seen that Leila's married!'

It was as if she wanted to say that at least no one could say anything bad about me now, unlike her daughter.

Souria's father was always at the mosque, so he didn't see what his daughter did during the day. In the evening, however, he hounded her for every little thing: her make-up, her clothes, her hair – and so did her brothers. One of them had officially been keeping her under surveillance since she'd been tied to her bed for that serious misdemeanour, and she was always on edge because of him. However, Souria's nature was different from mine; we'd had different upbringings and anyway she survived quite happily in this world governed by inquisition.

'Leila, don't let it get to you!' This was Souria's favourite expression, while I had been letting it get to me for years to the point of driving myself crazy. I wanted to stay 'single' for as long as possible, especially at the factory; I lied to myself as easily as breathing. Even when Moussa turned up at my home for two months, I acted as though he didn't exist. Some sort of family cousin.

My mother kept saying to me, 'Go and see your husband!'

'But I'm not married to him yet. Incidentally, when do I have to hand over my virginity?'

'On your wedding day.'

'Then, sorry, but I'm not yet married to him.'

'OK. And make sure you don't give him anything before your wedding day. If he tries telling you that you're his wife, don't listen to him!'

'No, I won't, don't worry, Maman.'

Another contradiction. 'Go and see your husband, but if he wants you to be his wife, refuse!'

Although my parents agreed with me for once on this point, it was because a paper husband could still change his mind after taking advantage of me and repudiate me. During this period, though, that argument helped me keep my distance from him, because he did ask me to sleep with him.

'You're my wife now. It doesn't matter whether we do it now or later.'

That day, I became sadistic.

'Do you love me?'

'Yes.'

'Do you love me enough to kiss my feet?'

'Yes, I'll kiss your feet, anything you like.'

'Go on then, I dare you!'

He did it, the idiot. My mother came into the lounge at that very moment.

'Do you realise how much a man who kisses your feet must really love you?'

Poor Maman. I didn't believe in Moussa's so-called love for a second.

However, at the time and in their defence, my parents didn't think that he was just marrying me to obtain his papers; he'd given them the same speech as he had me, saying, 'She can decide whether we live in France or Morocco.' He'd already stopped mentioning Spain, where he'd said he used to work. I've never known what he did there; he didn't have a residence permit over there at any rate.

I sent him off to sleep somewhere else, but he tried it on often enough, and as a girl doesn't talk about 'that' to her father (that would be 'shameful'), he knew I wouldn't complain. It was up to me to combat his advances.

'I'm not your wife yet, so don't touch me! What will I do on our wedding day if your mother asks me to show her the blood?'

'Don't worry about that! I'm the one who decides, no one else decides.'

Fortunately, we weren't left alone that often. I was still working, in the daytime, though, as the night work had dried up, and was alternating morning and afternoon shifts. In the morning I'd leave at 4.30 a.m. and came back at 1.30 p.m. In the afternoon I'd leave at noon and not be back before 9 p.m. However, as soon as he resumed the offensive, the prospect of that so-called 'wedding night' terrified me. I blocked out the unhappiness in store for me, as I'd always done.

The formal wedding in Morocco with its lavish reception was planned for the holidays, since my parents hadn't had the time to organise it in the winter. The wedding reception always costs a fortune and families traditionally run into debt to make it an unforgettable occasion. For some girls it may be the best day of their lives, but in my present state of mind I only saw the negative side.

Everything is analysed at this ceremony: the bride, the groom, how they met each other, the quality of the food, the jewellery and the dresses. The guests want to know every-thing, so they can tell people about it afterwards. You come in for constant criticism whatever you do. You could serve the guests their food on gold dishes and they'd still find something to criticise – even the way the bread is sliced.

They dissect everything. If the community doesn't know the groom or the bride, it's even worse. They examine them hair by hair. He's handsome, she's as ugly as sin or the other way round, and finally they pass judgement. This one's a fine figure of a man, that one looks like the back of a bus. The families, meanwhile, are assessed in terms of the money they've spent.

This is how reputations are made: what people say about a wedding travels from one family to another and malicious gossip spreads like wildfire. Sometimes the mothers end up with dreadful reputations as a result of this; after all, they are responsible for the 'window-dressing'.

'You know, Mrs so-and-so put on a third-rate wedding! In her shoes, frankly, I wouldn't have bothered to do anything at all because, to be perfectly honest, the whole evening was a complete shambles.'

Or else: 'She organised a French-style wedding; it would've been better if she'd done nothing at all!'

'French-style' means that the wedding is very simple, while 'Moroccan-style' means it could have come straight out of the *Arabian Nights*.

While waiting for the formal consecration ceremony that led to the wedding night, I'd found it easy to resist the sexual pressure exerted by my paper husband. Finally, however, I cracked, or to quote the actual words used: I had a nervous breakdown.

It was triggered by an unhappy event. One of my childhood friends had lost her father, a man I'd respected enormously. The traditional visit to offer my condolences was the first time I'd been in the presence of a dead man. I'd known the man all my life and felt as if an old world of hope had died with him.

A dead man's family always entertains a great many people. Tea is served to the visitors who are continually arriving and leaving, and all the girls help with tidying up and washing the dishes. Without realising it I was tidying up and washing and wiping dishes like crazy. As soon as there was a glass, I needed to wash, wash, wash. At a certain point I began to think I was going mad.

No one realised I wasn't feeling well; I began to feel dizzy. I felt as if I was suffocating and needed to get some air. I tried to joke about my discomfort with one of my friends. 'Mina! I'm really hyper! Someone must've slipped me one of those drugs that cyclists take!'

Although she laughed, she thought I looked pale, so she took me out into the hallway of her flats for a rest, but I felt increasingly ill sitting on the stairs. My head grew heavier and heavier until it became too heavy to hold up.

'Mina, I don't feel well, I don't feel well . . . '

'Stop it, you're starting to freak me out.'

She began to joke around, talking about djinns, spirits of the dead who were taking over my mind.

Suddenly I started to laugh hysterically and I had the distinct feeling that I was losing touch with reality. I was mad, they'd taken over my mind, my legs no longer supported me, they'd destroyed me, this time I couldn't go on fighting for my survival, I had come to the end of my tether. Mina was in a panic when she saw me looking so stricken, so she took me back inside. I went into the bathroom to splash water on my face, walking like a zombie, heavy shoulders dragging a body that could no longer support the weight of my head.

As I was raising my head from the basin, I suddenly felt as if I'd been thrown against the wall by a gust of wind, even though I hadn't moved an inch, and I fell to the floor. It was incredibly violent. I curled into a foetal ball, incapable of talking, even though I was screaming. I was convinced that my mouth wasn't in the right place any more: it was the wrong way up. That's what traumatised me the most – and also the fact that I could no longer feel my feet. I was having an attack of tetany for the first time in my life, an attack that lasted the rest of the day and a whole night, because no one called a doctor. They thought I'd fallen prey to spirits. The imam read the Koran, they threw water over me while I was raving and everyone thought I was possessed. I was actually talking about the dead in my delirium, saying that they were all around me, that they had to be stopped from stealing my soul.

With hindsight I think that subconsciously I wanted to die and be delivered from this life, which was giving me none of the peace and happiness I would have expected at my age. I didn't try to understand it any more than that or indulge in any two-bit psychology; that would have meant getting treatment and that was out of the question. Spirits are not available for consultation by a doctor . . .

Mina told me all about this, because I don't remember anything except for the tornado that hurled me onto the floor, depriving me of the use of my feet, with my mouth the wrong way up and my body curled in a ball.

When I came to my senses, I was still terrified by that horrible experience and I hoped I'd never go through it again. Unfortunately, it reoccurred later.

I thought I was mad. I was ashamed to go and see the doctor because he would have asked questions, tried to find out what wasn't going well in my life, and he knew my parents, the whole family. He didn't know that I'd been married by force and that I was afraid people would think badly of my parents if he diagnosed that my 'illness' had been caused by the marriage.

I was trapping myself in shame and humiliation, incapable of imagining that someone might be able to help me and save me from outside. That's what non-Muslims don't understand. They have recourse to the medical profession who, in my case, would have diagnosed a psychosomatic reaction, a nervous breakdown, a calcium and magnesium deficiency, or the need for psychological help, while my family was still light years away from contemplating anything like that. Unfortunately, we still harbour thoughts of djinns, curses and devilish enchantments that invade the bodies of rebellious women. My attack had no medical name at that time. As far as I was concerned, I was just going mad; in my family's opinion, the spirits were out to get me.

After studying my case the people around me came to the

conclusion that I was betrothed and not yet married, and should therefore never have entered the house of a dead man. A virgin is easy prey for bad spirits. They want to possess her. It's even said that a spirit can 'marry' the body of a virgin.

There are male and female spirits. People make them do what suits them. If someone has cracked and needs a shrink, they say, 'Poor man, he's possessed.' It's cultural. There are psychiatrists in Morocco, but only for raving lunatics, the ones who are locked away in an asylum. The others, those who are so depressed that they cannot talk any more and let themselves die, they are the ones who are possessed.

So the other women blamed my mother. 'Why did you let her come here? Why did you let her kiss the forehead of a dead man?'

I had to stop work. I'd come to the end of my tether. I had become anorexic and had even stopped drinking liquids. I was having two or three fits of hysterics a week, so I decided to go to the doctor, virtually in secret. Reason: fatigue. Verdict: nervous breakdown. The antidepressants helped me to resurface in a strange way. I was spaced out so I no longer worried about anything. I felt fine in my muffled world; I didn't give a damn about anything else. I was sleeping all the time and I was happy, but not at all clear-headed: I was completely out of it. Moreover, I was getting thinner and thinner: there was nothing of me; I was just skin and bones. I'd told my parents that the doctor had given me vitamins. They wouldn't have accepted a nervous breakdown and I was afraid my father might take my medication away from me, that magic potion which was setting me free. In his view an antidepressant is a drug. There's no such thing as depression.

So I was forced to lie and to hide the pills that were helping me regain my sanity, but I was losing it so badly that I was no longer taking anything in. One day I had an absolutely un-believable fit of hysterics. My parents had moved me into their bedroom so that I could have some peace and quiet; that wretched room which recalled such humiliating memories. People were parading through the house as if they were visit-ing a dying woman under the pretext of finding out how I was; they wanted to see with their own eyes if I'd been taken over by the spirits or not. I was lying in bed, feeling desper-ately unhappy; just opposite me the wedding dress was hanging on a coat hanger on the door. All the wedding gifts were strewn around me for that fabulous morning when I would become a woman.

I stared at the extremely expensive wedding dress. I walked into the kitchen like a zombie and picked up a knife; I wanted to murder that dress. But my mother saw me and followed me into the bedroom. I was already holding the dress, ready to shred it to pieces, when she caught my arm, calling to my father for help. It took five or six of them to control me, to hold my legs and arms. I was hitting everything I could and everything was a blur. I just wanted one thing: to rip that bloody wedding dress to shreds. I wanted it to die so that I wouldn't have to look at it any more.

This time I had clearly fallen prey to black magic. They no longer thought spirits possessed me: someone had put a curse on me. Curses hold a prominent place in our culture and everyone speaks about them in whispers, sure that they exist. They didn't know who had put the curse on me, but I had to be placed in the hands of an exorcist, someone capable of removing the curse.

Many people say they've fallen victim to a curse or are said to have been cursed. Who puts curses on people? It can be a mother-in-law who wants to dispose of her daughter-in-law, a maidservant who wants to marry her boss, etc. All kinds of people may cast a curse. In my case I would have found it hard to suspect anyone. It was, however, clear to everyone around me that the real Leila no longer existed. I was not able to control my mind or body anymore: they were possessed by a devil.

In the meantime, having been saved in the nick of time, my wedding dress was put somewhere safe, and I eventually calmed down and fell into an exhausted sleep. My mother told me that I got up during the night and that she found me just about to climb over the balcony. Fortunately, she'd been watching me. My father locked the balcony and they kept me under constant supervision after that.

That was the day my father found my medication when he was going through my things. He called the doctor, who told him gravely, 'Monsieur, your daughter is in the middle of a serious nervous breakdown. She must take this medication.'

'No, this is a drug! It's out of the question for my daughter to take this filth; one thing has nothing to do with the other.'

The doctor wasn't able to do anything.

I'd lost touch with reality. I was vaguely watching things happening around me, feeling as if I was dead, and no one suspected a thing. I was buried in a tomb; the fly couldn't even see through the glass; it was all too much, much too much. The closer the wedding came, the crazier I became. I lacked the survival instinct and anger that can save you. I was slipping into depressive madness. The next day I had another attack and I no longer had any medication. There were two of us in my body. A real split personality.

All this happened some time before the lavish wedding in Morocco. Moussa was coming to collect us. My parents' first priority was to make sure that he didn't find out about my condition. He might have called off the marriage and repudiated me. I might have been saved from great unhappiness, but at the cost of disgracing my parents. Repudiated, divorced, it didn't matter – it would have been recorded in the Aduls' great ledger and no one would ever have been able to swear that this daughter was a virgin again. I didn't even think about that. I was crying in the silence, in the desert, but no one heard me.

I'd broken off communication with my friends. I saw Souria less and less. Before the marriage I met up with people, laughed, managed to live. During that period I cut myself off and withdrew into myself.

The attacks become more and more frequent. My father triggered one of them. He'd just tried to be affectionate by hugging me without saying anything. I'll never know what he was thinking or what he couldn't say to me, because I began screaming, 'Don't touch me. Don't you dare touch me!'

I pushed him away with incredible strength given that I was as light as a feather. I was cross with myself later, because that was what I'd always wanted, my father cuddling me, comforting me, protecting me, showing he loved me without a broom handle or taboos and obligations.

It was too late. I'd pushed him away, screaming blue murder. I was really acting as if I were possessed by the devil. I burst out laughing, I wept, I screamed, 'Maman! Papa!'

Was I begging them for help? Was I rejecting them? I have no idea.

If only my father had just sat down beside me, and said, 'We're calling the whole thing off. I'm not making you marry anyone any more.'

My brothers and my mother came to the rescue; they pounced on me and pinned me to the floor. I was screaming and giggling at the same time. I felt as if I was physically sinking into the floor, as if I was being sucked under. When a friend of the family, who was a nurse, saw me like this, she said to my father, 'She has to be taken to hospital. She's completely dehydrated and, anyway, she's obviously having a fit of hysterics.'

'No, no, there's nothing to worry about. We've got everything under control.'

My mother immediately went into the kitchen to make something to eat, to force me to swallow something. Nothing doing. I was letting myself die and the nurse knew it. My parents refused to take me to the hospital. As far as they were concerned, doctors couldn't heal me.

It was serious, but I can't bear any hard feelings towards them now. My condition went far beyond their comprehension. They grew up within that culture, that tradition, and they did what they could in the belief that they were doing the right thing. At the time I wouldn't have said that. I often felt hatred and anger towards them and I detested them. I felt as if I were dying of hunger, despair and helpless rebellion. I could see myself disappearing; I don't know whether anyone else has experienced that giddy sensation of being pursued by death, that terrible fear of vanishing under the ground.

The neighbours came to the rescue. A girl in their family had cracked because she'd been married by force. They'd come across the problem and had taken her to an imam who was a healer. So they had to take me there right away. My trip there bordered on the surreal, although it really happened. My father carried me over his shoulder like a bag. I could see he was unhappy because he was crying. But it was too late for me. I had been driven mad and was full of hate; he had destroyed me and was still desperately trying to destroy me. My father's tears didn't in the least affect me.

I found myself in the house of that famous imam, who took charge of me immediately. He ushered me into a room and wouldn't allow my parents in. He knew what he was doing and, before anyone confuses him with a real imam, I'd rather say outright that, unfortunately for me and all the women and young girls he was treating, this so-called religious man was actually a lousy crook.

He made me lie on the floor and picked up a sabre. He asked me to uncover my stomach, and then lower down. A religious man would never have done that, but he knew he was safe because he worked behind closed doors and because girls don't talk about 'these things'.

He pressed the sabre hard against my stomach, almost hard enough to draw blood, while invoking something or other. I didn't understand a word he was saying. He put some herbs in a brazier to create some smoke, and then straddled my chest and began to slap me violently and systematically, while shouting in Arabic, 'You will leave her body! Are you a Muslim? Are you a Jew? Are you a Christian? Are you an atheist?'

He kept on slapping me with all his might, a slap, then an order, 'Leave her body or I'll burn you!'

Then he picked up a hot coal with a long pair of tongs and threatened my stomach.

I don't know how, but I had a flash of clarity at that moment. I couldn't stand it any longer. My face was purple with the blows, my skin bore the marks of that maniac's large hands, and my nose was black and blue; even my own father had never hit me like that. To top it all, he was being paid to do it. He wanted to burn my stomach and I saw the tongs, the red-hot coal that was going to scorch me, while he screamed, 'Leave her body!'

So I screamed, 'Yes, yes!'

As if I were taking the place of the spirit.

It was instinctive. I no longer had my wits about me. I was defending myself as best I could.

'You're sure you will leave her body?'

'Yes . . . yes . . . I'm leaving!'

This was madness. Did he really think he was talking to a spirit?

There was only one way out, only one way to escape from his filthy clutches: I had to play along with him. Otherwise, I was done for. I was afraid of dying, afraid of suffering, afraid that he'd burn me or that he'd go on hitting me. So I stood up and walked out of the room and he didn't stop me.

It wasn't much help to me, this demon business. My mother, who was firmly convinced of it, greeted me in tears.

'Oh, my daughter, I've got my daughter back!'

That bastard had stumbled across a real money-spinner; my mother gave him 1,000 francs.

My parents asked whether they needed to bring me back. Obviously he wasn't about to say no. I was a little more lucid after that ridiculous episode, but still exhausted. I was walking very slowly and couldn't bear the slightest noise, but I could see that his waiting room was filled with people willing to dip into their wallets.

My father was waiting with the neighbour and his daughter Azra. When she saw me come out, she fainted and the crook took advantage of that to tell her father, 'Your daughter is still possessed. You must bring her back to see me!'

He'd made mincemeat of me; I didn't recognise myself when I looked in the mirror. However, I had been carried like a sack to see that maniac and I was walking on the way back, so the maniac had won. Once again I had been humiliated, and I had to go back for a complete cure.

I didn't want to see anyone. I was still not eating and hardly drinking; my body had decided to let itself die. Two days later I was forced to get up and go back to see the imam.

I knew what he was capable of and did my best to keep my wits about me.

'So, how are you?'

'I'm fine.'

Then he spoke to my parents who, of course, had told him everything about me. 'Someone has cast a spell on her to make her reject her husband! I shall take care of it. But next time, you must bring me a black cockerel to be slaughtered. You'll take your daughter to a bridge so that she can throw it into the current! She'll turn her back on the river and throw it over her shoulder!'

I found it hard to imagine myself on a bridge over the Seine, swinging a blood-soaked cockerel above my head. Then I was again locked with him in that room, which was furnished with a large bed.

He spoke, debating all on his own; all I wanted to do was to get out of there as fast as possible. Suddenly he said, 'Lie down!'

'No, I'm fine . . . I don't need to lie down.'

I sat down warily on a corner of the bed. He stood in front of me.

'Stand up now. Do you love your husband?'

'Of course I love him.'

'Are you sure? I'm not. Someone has done something to you to make you hate him. Now I'm going to make you love him. You will look at me and see your husband-to-be in me.'

He moved closer to me and held me tightly.

'Do you see your husband in me?'

He rubbed himself against me as I was standing there; I could smell him, his sex. He kissed me on the mouth. I was paralysed with fright and I couldn't scream. Anyway, there were 15 people as well as my parents in the waiting room. Scream what? Rape? No one would have believed me; a crook like that doesn't rape a girl. He knows she must remain a virgin, but nothing and no one prevents him from taking advantage of her, while asking for more money. The girl is never going to run out of that room to tell her parents that he touched her. An imam?

It was unbearably humiliating; that disgusting old man with his white djellaba and his turban, that so-called religious man, whom my parents trusted to the point of placing me in his hands without knowing him, was in the process of subjecting me to what was obviously a sexual assault. In the name of what? Why me? Again? What on earth had I done to all these men?

Then he ordered me to lie down and went through the same old rigmarole with the sabre over my lower abdomen. With hindsight I tell myself that all he could do was to rub himself up against me like a pig and ogle me like a dirty old man. In the meantime, however, I had to submit to his insulting behaviour in silence and I would happily have slit his throat.

I had noticed a 14-year-old girl with her parents in his waiting room. I'd heard them tell my mother, 'Someone has cast a spell on her to make her go out with boys, sully her parents' honour and lose her virginity.'

Another girl was there because her husband had left her and she wanted a 'spell' to make him come back to her. That poor kid was almost certainly going to go through what I did, and so were others, but he probably wouldn't assault a married woman. Mind you . . .

I choked back my hatred. 'OK, we can call my parents now.'

I never talked about this to anyone; that guy had carte blanche. He went to the mosque, he led the prayer, and he was officially a good Muslim and a fervent fundamentalist. If I had dared to accuse him, I would have placed myself in danger. Whatever happens, whatever is done to us, we have to keep quiet and they know it. I caught the eye of the young girl as I left the room into which she would be going next – he was going to do the same to her too. I could have vomited with disgust and shame. That poor girl was only trying to go out and have a little fun, like me.

I had to put up with that sex maniac for five sessions. In the third session he made me drink some sort of potion; I had to swallow down three bottles of the stuff, nearly three pints, without throwing up. I don't know what it was: foul, bitter brown water with herbs. I threw up violently, sick as a dog. On the fourth occasion he began his performance again.

'Do you see your husband in me?'

I said yes very quickly . . .

Then he slit the throat of the cockerel in his back yard, letting the blood flow into a pail. He dipped the poor cockerel in it and told my father to take me to a bridge to perform the ritual.

To my mother, he said, 'As for you, get a bucket and wash my back yard and house from top to bottom.'

The spell was supposed to leave along with the water wrung out of the cloth. This crafty 'spell' was hiding all over the place. That crook was treating himself to a charlady, who was actually paying him.

When we came out my father began looking for a bridge from which I could toss the blood-soaked cockerel. It's not easy to do something like that discreetly. There were always people around, even in the suburbs. We were all afraid, even my father. Eventually he parked in a virtually deserted area and made me get out of the car on my own. Holding the cockerel by the legs, I started walking, looking around, and quickly threw the bird into the Seine.

I can still see myself on that bridge, a frightened girl, broken, thin and wraithlike, tossing that obnoxious thing into the river. I can laugh about it now, saying to myself that I might have thrown it in too hastily . . .

In the meantime, my husband-to-be had arrived and made himself comfortable at home. Moussa came with us for the fifth session, since the crook had said he had to see what he looked like. Fortunately, Moussa wasn't fooled. I wasn't in love with him, but I must admit that he was perceptive at least about this. All the same, he played along. The other man gave him a lecture of sorts. 'Pay attention, you must look after her carefully; she's the daughter of a good family.'

'Yes . . . yes, OK.'

I wanted to grab the imam by the throat and punch him in the face. The daughter of a good family, whom you've abused, you dirty old man. Moussa gazed at him mockingly. He saw my mother handing him some money and patted her on the shoulder.

'I see he's found some real suckers.'

He had seen I was in a terrible state physically and I even think he pitied me a little. I was unrecognisable; he told my parents so. He didn't call off the marriage, nevertheless. He could never for a moment have imagined what that freak had put me through. I couldn't tell him either. Anyway, I think he would have married me on a stretcher . . .

The final piece of advice from the sorcerer, who could see that my husband-to-be didn't believe his nonsense, was designed to scare him. He said to my parents, 'A "curse" has been put on the two of them and it's very likely that they will separate after the wedding if you don't do what I tell you to do. When you slit the throat of the sheep on the wedding day, keep its head and place it in the wedding hall, high up so that it's always looking down on the couple. Put this piece of paper in the sheep's mouth, under its tongue, to ensure they are both protected.'

I could just see the blood-soaked sheep's head with its lolling tongue adorned with a paper talisman on which he'd written the devil knows what in the reception room of the grand hotel my father had hired for the occasion. All this was a crock of blood, sexuality, bullshit and crazy morbidity. Even in Morocco I'd never heard of such a thing.

Despite being a physical and mental wreck, I couldn't help laughing when my mother said as we came out, 'We must do it. We must do it.'

'But it's complete bullshit.'

'No, it isn't. You must believe in it so that everything will go smoothly.'

She has always firmly believed in the powers of that charlatan. She even tried to go back to see him later, but he'd disappeared without a forwarding address. Gone to the devil. I hope.

Although he didn't say it, Moussa was perfectly aware of my desperate rejection and he was obviously not going to give way. He had the law on his side now: whether I liked it or not,

I had become his wife before the Aduls. I was officially forced to recover from my nervous breakdown by myself to avoid returning to that pervert, who was capable of beating me. I forced myself to eat a little, but I really needed treatment and to talk to someone normal, who didn't regard my fits of hysterics as the result of a curse. Unfortunately, that wasn't allowed.

It was soon time for the wedding preparations and our departure for Morocco – the trip in an overcrowded car, our arrival with the family and my immediate imprisonment.

My father: 'You're forbidden to go out at all; you're betrothed to a man!'

Most importantly, no one was supposed to see me outside the house, so I was kept incarcerated for a fortnight before the lavish reception that brought about financial ruin and debt, if need be, to ensure my unhappiness. That's how it is – you have to bankrupt yourself even if it's for your daughter's forced marriage.

Apart from my parents and me, everyone thought that this was a happy wedding desired by everyone. I cried my eyes out during this period: someone said 'good morning' and I cried; 'good evening' and I cried.

I was on the home straight and my father kept pestering me. 'Don't go out on the balcony, don't go out on the terrace; you mustn't be seen.'

One day – a Wednesday as I remember – my parents went to visit my grandfather in the mountains and I was left in charge of the house. Moussa took advantage of the situation to spend the night there. He was my lord and master and it was up to him to keep an eye on me. I went up onto the terrace, smoked a cigarette and, when I came down, I went to sit beside him, reeking of tobacco. I even kissed him to make sure he smelled it. In Morocco a woman who smokes is indecent – even more indecent than in my neighbourhood.

I wanted to provoke him, even though I'd stopped smoking ages ago, but he didn't say anything; he was just in a bad mood with me. However, the next day he counter-attacked.

'I thought you were the daughter of a good family, but you smoke!'

'Yes, it's a shame, isn't it? I forgot to tell you.'

'Tomorrow, it's over. We'll stop everything. I don't want a wife who smokes cigarettes!'

If only I could've shouted, 'Yeah! Great! I'm going to smoke four packets of fags a day until you clear out of the house!'

I had a spark of hope (but at what cost?) when my parents came back, and said, 'Where's Moussa?'

'He left. We had a row; he doesn't want to marry me anymore.'

My father dashed over to the telephone and Moussa denounced me, saying, 'Your daughter isn't the girl I believed she was. I thought she was a girl from a good family, but it seems that she smokes cigarettes. She smoked in front of me yesterday.'

My father was beside himself with anger. He asked Moussa to come over with his brothers and his father. I was in the kitchen. I took refuge in a corner, but he beat me: slaps, insults, and kicks. I was given a thrashing, just like before. 'You're nothing but a tart!'

Family council. Once again, I found myself hauled before the justice of men and I had another attack of tetany. Moussa had never seen me in this condition and was a little panicked by it. I was taken into a bedroom and they continued to discuss their business, in other words, me and cigarettes, while my mother tried to look after me. I had been beaten and Moussa had absolutely no intention of annulling the marriage. He simply wanted to show my father that his daughter had scored low marks, to humiliate him so that he'd apologise for giving him a bad daughter like me and not a rare pearl. It was just play-acting.

Naturally, I was told nothing about their discussions. My father only came into the room to threaten me. 'I'm warning you, if you don't stop all this nonsense, I'll slit your throat. I'll slit your throat.'

This was just to put me in my place. Parents know that they are dominating their daughters, and the words they use are violent. At the time, however, I still wondered if he was capable of seeing it through to the bitter end. My resistance was just one more detail to sort out.

However, misery doesn't give a damn about details. He dragged me to the forced marriage like a sheep to the slaughter.

CHAPTER SEVEN

About happiness

THAT WRETCHED FRIDAY, THE day of celebration, had arrived. I'd been taken to the hotel booked by my father, the lavish festivities were about to start and I no longer had any way of defending myself, so I sulked and refused to speak to my fiancé.

'Stop sulking, everyone can see.'

'If I want to sulk, I'll sulk. Whose business is it anyway?'

Inwardly, I was saying, 'I hate you and I want to show everyone that I hate you, even if you are achieving your objective.'

He left me with the dressers, the make-up artists and the hairdressers. I had to wear nine different outfits during the course of the same evening. A good average – some brides wear as many as 20. For my first appearance, I wore a white kaftan with an imitation diamond tiara and earrings. I was taken round the back of the hotel, so that no one would see me before the official entrance of the bride enthroned on a golden palanquin. It was a royal entrance. I was carried in like a wondrous princess from the *Arabian Nights*.

The wife-to-be must radiate beauty, even if she's ugly. She

must wave as she goes by, like the Queen of England, smiling to the right and left. I felt ridiculous, awkward. If I'd been in love and at peace with myself, I would have loved making the most of that magical time in a woman's life. Adorned with finery, beautifully made-up, dripping with jewellery and admired by everyone: it must be an exhilarating feeling. Instead, I felt stupid with a tense smile on my face, thinking, 'What the hell am I doing here?'

I was being suffocated by this sudden plunge into the traditional world from which I'd more or less escaped in France, going to school wearing jeans and trainers. All those beatings for trying to escape had been for nothing; I was back to square one like everyone else. So I paraded all those different dresses – the blue, the white, the pink, the green, the Indian outfit, and the pharaoh's costume. No danger of me forgetting that one: it must have weighed at least 40 pounds and was designed to make you look like a majestic peacock. All the dresses belonged to a professional who hired herself out complete with her gear and her team.

The pharaoh's costume was the last outfit before the wedding dress – the famous dress that had cost my parents a fortune and I'd wanted to slash to pieces. For her last appearance the bride throws sugar almonds from the palanquin. She will soon disappear with her husband. The wedding night happens the morning after a night of performances, forced smiles and enthusiastic whoops.

My French friends who had been invited to my wedding thought this lavish ceremony was like a dream from some fairytale. They had never seen the other side of the coin. Naturally, everyone thought I looked fantastic, even Moussa, who said, 'You look wonderful!'

At the end of that long, torturous night, in the early hours of the morning, I was ushered into a smart car to take me to another hotel, to a room where I was finally going to give this virtual stranger the 'treasure of my virginity'.

Just as I climbed into the car, my youngest brother ran up with his hands shoved in his pockets and an inquisitive, rather unhappy expression on his face.

'Where are you going?'

I didn't know what to say to a ten-year-old boy; I was in tears.

'I'm going into town, to the hotel.'

'Everyone's going to sleep now; it's morning! Why aren't you coming home?'

'Because I'm married now.'

'But you're not allowed to leave just like that! Have you asked Papa?'

He had tears in his eyes. Had I asked Papa?

'You know, that was all I wanted, not to leave!'

'But you're going to come home.'

'Of course I'll come home, just not now.'

Ten years old, still innocent and the only one crying for me.

My father wasn't there when I was about to leave. I didn't know he was so exhausted that he'd fallen asleep on the spot. I looked around for him desperately.

I was crying like a little girl, calling for him to come and help me one last time. He finally arrived and hugged me tightly as he'd never really done before. I collapsed against him, crying. Everyone watching was moved because I looked like a girl from a good family, weeping with emotion at leaving the father who had always protected her.

I found myself in a large hotel room, the door locked on

my distress. There was no escape. Fortunately, he wasn't rough.

Two days after the wedding night, during which I had hardly bled, I woke up in the morning in a blood-soaked bed.

Moussa had gone off somewhere the night before, leaving me alone at my in-laws' house where, as custom dictates, I was supposed to live. I didn't have a stomach ache, I hadn't felt anything and I'd lost a dreadful amount of blood even though I wasn't due to have my period. I was shivering with fever and felt icy, and I was semi-conscious. I didn't know what to do, frightened by all that blood. It wasn't my mother-in-law who came up to the room to help me, but my father-in-law, who was concerned that he hadn't seen me emerge. He called Moussa's brothers and they wrapped me in some blankets, but I was still trembling with cold, so he sent one of his sons to fetch a doctor. He was a kind man and so were my brothers-in-law; they did everything they could to help and support me. The doctor couldn't visit the house so I had to be taken to see him in a taxi. My mother-in-law finally showed her face, furious at her husband.

'Don't do that with those blankets! They're brand new! Why did you get them out for her!'

She hadn't liked me on sight.

'A taxi? Not on your life! She's only been here two days! What if something happened to her? Phone her parents and tell them to deal with her!'

They rushed over, and as my poor mother hurried through their front door, she fell flat on her back. She was in so much pain that my father lost his temper.

'I don't believe this! It's one thing after another. I'm sick and tired of it!'

When she saw the pool of blood, she totally panicked,

thinking I was going to die. Much later she confided to me that she had been wondering – it was high time – whether this marriage had been a good thing. Too many bad omens . . .

My mother-in-law only had one thought: I was a snob. I hadn't come down to see her since I'd been in that room, I'd sulked during the wedding and her husband had taken seven new blankets out of their plastic covers to wrap round me. She'd had enough! I could die, but not in her house.

The doctor gave me an injection to stop the bleeding, which he couldn't explain.

My mother wanted to know if her son-in-law had been rough the first time, but there hadn't been any sign of violence and I knew how to recognise it better than anyone. At least I'd been lucky enough not to be landed with a sex maniac. Even if I didn't love him, I couldn't accuse him of anything.

I had to stay in bed for five days without getting up at all and my husband wasn't allowed to touch me for at least two weeks. I now know why I started to bleed like that. It was subconscious, but I'd already thought as much at the time. I was given a fortnight's holiday, granted officially by a doctor. It was the only way to be on my own in bed. My body was saying it for me. When you're not allowed to speak out or escape, you defend yourself as best you can, and the most effective way of putting some distance between you and a husband you don't want is to start bleeding.

I was taken back to my husband's family and my father-in-law decided to put me in a room on the ground floor with everybody else. He thought he was doing the right thing. 'We're going to stop isolating the poor girl; she can be near us.'

But I wasn't at home. My mother would have been more than happy to take care of me at home, but that was unthinkable: I was married, so I had to live with my husband's family, with people I didn't know and who I didn't want to know, especially my mother-in-law.

A very elderly lady came in and stretched out alongside me on the bed – Moussa's maternal grandmother.

'Are you Moussa's wife? Are you OK?'

'More or less.'

'You know, they're not very kind.'

'Why?'

'Because they're not very kind. That's just the way it is.'

She took my hand and looked at a gold-plated ring, which wasn't terribly valuable.

'That's a pretty ring . . . you know, I've never had a ring in my life.'

'Here, you can have this.'

I slid the ring onto her finger, and she said, 'Thank you, my dear, thank you.'

She started telling me about her own daughter, my mother-in-law. I realised that no one paid any attention to her because she was too old, poor sighted and a burden. My feelings about my mother-in-law were confirmed. Someone who doesn't love her own mother . . . I was a stranger to the family; she was hardly going to do me any favours.

She also told me about her granddaughter, Moussa's sister. 'She's a nasty piece of work, so you'd better watch out for her; she's really vicious and she'll make you suffer. She'll do anything she can to hurt you, so protect yourself, my girl, protect yourself and watch out.'

At that moment she saw her coming through the French window. 'Shhh, the battleaxe is coming.'

I pretended to be asleep while the other woman scolded her grandmother. 'What the hell are you doing here? Get back to your room!'

'No, I'm fine here.'

But she had seen the ring and reported back to her mother, which caused a ridiculous mini-scandal that very evening.

Moussa came to see me at my bedside, and said, 'Leila, did you give that ring to my grandmother?'

'Yes, I did; it was a gift!'

'OK, but it's causing all kinds of problems and my mother has taken the ring.'

'Your mother took the ring! Then, to avoid any problems, go and tell her that Leila simply put it on the old lady's finger and forgot about it.'

From then on, my mother-in-law began to regard me with great hostility and I counted the days until I could go back home to my family.

As soon as I could get up, I went to visit my parents and then I went to have my hair cut at the hairdresser's, without asking anyone. That brought me into conflict with my mother-in-law.

'You've had your hair cut! You should've asked your husband's permission.'

'Your daughters-in-law also have their hair cut; that hasn't caused any problems . . . '

'Yes, but you must always ask permission before you do something.'

My father-in-law cut her short, saying, 'Mind your own business and let her live her life; she'll sort all that out with her husband if it really is a problem. Leave her alone.'

For once, I had a man's support, but my mother-in-law became increasingly hostile towards me.

I felt better, lighter with shorter hair, but Moussa wouldn't tolerate it. His mother, I suppose, had got him all worked up about it, saying something along the lines of, 'She's only been your wife for a week and she's already doing what she wants. She's been to have her hair cut and she went to visit her parents without asking permission. When you're not here she must ask my permission! You'll never control her!'

She used the classic expression used by a typical mother-in-law for the benefit of her beloved son: 'You won't *control* her!'

He was in a real mood when he came in. 'Who gave you permission to have your hair cut?'

'The day you met me I had short hair, didn't I? I let it grow for the wedding, because I was asked to do so. Now the wedding is over I can have my hair cut.'

'Now that you're married and you're a man's wife, you must wear your hair tied back.'

'Perhaps, but I've had it cut. Do you want to try and stick it back on?'

After splitting hairs like this, he continued talking about the principle. I wasn't to visit my parents without asking permission either from him or his mother. I began arguing, and then, fed up with fighting, lost my temper. 'From your mother? Who am I married to? Your mother or you?'

'There's no difference! When I'm not here, it's my mother.'

'Excuse me, but I'm not married to Mrs what's-her-name! I signed a contract with you! If his lordship doesn't trust his wife then he should tell her!'

I'd decided not to let him have the upper hand from the start. Neither he nor his mother were going to give me orders. I'd been ordered about enough. During the three-week honeymoon on the Mediterranean coast, I worked off my frustration by taking a string of petty revenges. Let him pay – through the nose. Another ring, earrings, clothes galore . . . He'd selected a decent hotel, but I wanted a more expensive one and I got it. It was that or nothing.

'Who do you think I am? A government minister?'

I was demanding and indifferent. I wanted him to empty his wallet. Since I'd been 'sold' to that man, so to speak – that was really how I felt about it at the time anyway – he had to pay. It was stupid, but it made me feel better. The sun, the sea, the narrow streets with no cars, and the souks in the old town – I enjoyed that magnificent region, its colours and scents. I knew my return to France would be difficult. We were going to live with my parents in part of the lounge screened off by a curtain until a partition could be made; he wouldn't be able to look for a job until he had a residence permit. I wondered what he was going to do. Sponge off my parents?

We went before the Mayor, which was a necessary formality for him. I climbed the steps of the town hall and said 'yes' with a heavy heart. It had to be done but I felt terribly sad. This was followed by the race for his papers: first a residence permit, which he obtained easily, and then, after a year of living together, he could apply for French nationality. A year's not very long to become French by marriage.

The year went past without too many crises. I looked for work since we couldn't help my parents make ends meet just with unemployment benefit, but unfortunately couldn't find anything and being stuck at home with an extra spy on my back infuriated me. One day I had renewed hope that I might be able to kick him out. We had opened a joint account at the bank, naturally, and he used to open the post, naturally . . . I glanced absent-mindedly at the bank statement he'd just laid on the breakfast table and noticed a line: 'Payment from Miss so-and-so . . . the sum of . . . '

I hadn't looked deliberately. I hadn't suspected him of anything before that, but he folded up the document very quickly, which aroused my suspicions, so I seized my opportunity.

'Give me that!'

I ran into my father's bedroom, screaming, 'Is this honesty, is this fidelity? He's getting money from some slut!'

If I'd dared to do that before I was married, I would have been given a good hiding, but my father's attitude towards me had changed and he could see from the statement that I was telling the truth. He also realised what I had realised: my husband was probably being unfaithful to me. Moussa had taken refuge in the lounge and was silently sulking. My mother, still worried that this husband might repudiate her daughter, said, 'That's enough. You've annoyed him.'

'How come I've annoyed him? Some girlfriend is paying money into his account. I don't know where she's come from, and I'm what? A stupid idiot?'

I went back in to challenge him, followed by my parents; I thought they were going to support me this time in view of the proof I had in my hands.

'Sweetheart, if you want to go and be with Miss what's-her-name who's giving you money, then go to her: that would suit me fine!'

But my mother turned against me. 'You shouldn't talk to your husband like that. You're entitled to try and understand, but nicely.'

Moussa stammered out some implausible explanation. A friend owed him money and his sister had paid him back instead. I didn't believe it for a second.

'Of course, that explains it! Why not go on taking me for an idiot?'

'Leila! If your husband tells you something, you must trust him!'

Maman . . . I adore my mother, but I couldn't tolerate this constant submissiveness, this need to worship men at all costs. They're right, we must trust them, believe them even if they're lying, so that they won't run off and leave us flat, repudiated, the laughing stock of the neighbourhood, the family, the country of our ancestors.

After a year my husband had not been looking for work so he hadn't found any, but I had found myself a job. I was working as a nanny for a French family. The job came with accommodation, so for the first time in my life I was living away from home all week. I only came back at the weekend.

While waiting for his papers, Moussa received his pocket money from my mother and he had board and lodging. Eventually, though, he decided to join me in the small studio flat that went with my job, and spent his time loitering around the streets of Paris.

I really made an effort to get used to him; I even pretended to be in love with him to see if I could fall in love for real. I lied to myself for some time, persuading myself that I needed to learn how to love him. It didn't get me anywhere.

He wanted to do a training course. It didn't matter what, as long as he was being paid for doing nothing. He had no ambitions or plans for the future. All he thought about was sending money to his mother, while I worked my fingers to the bone. One day he decided to go and visit her – he was missing her too badly.

She used to phone him from time to time. One day he was

out, and I answered the phone instead. After the usual cour-
tesies, I politely asked how she was.

'Dear, oh dear . . . my knee is so painful, my girl! I need to
go and see a specialist.'

In other words: if you have any money, you should send it
to me.

'I'm suffering from water retention and they're going to
drain it.'

'That's not serious.'

'I know, but I'm in so much pain, it hurts so badly! Tell my
son I phoned.'

'Yes, of course. Say hello to everyone.'

I hung up and I forgot to tell Moussa when he came in. It
was only when we were sitting down to eat that I remembered
the phone call.

'Oh, I forgot to tell you, your mother phoned. She has
fluid on her knee and they're going to drain it.'

You'd have thought I'd announced that his mother was
dying. He pushed back his plate, put his head in his hands and
began to cry. My mother stared at him wide-eyed. My father
glanced at me out of the corner of his eye, his teeth clenched.
I couldn't see what was so dramatic about all of this.

'So what? Fluid on the knee isn't serious! It can be
removed!'

In the heavy silence, I made matters worse. 'Maman! Your
friend Saida had fluid drained and she didn't die!'

My father exploded. 'Shut up, or you'll get this plate over
your head!'

My mother said sympathetically, 'Eat, Moussa.'

'No, I've lost my appetite.'

Me, angrily, 'Why don't you eat? This is bullshit – your
mother isn't going to die!'

I continued eating quietly, so he stood up from the table and went to sob his heart out in our room. Unbelievable. My mother was cross.

'Are you satisfied? Well, are you satisfied now?'

'But, Maman, this is over nothing! Nothing at all! She hasn't got cancer, after all!'

'That's not the point! It's the principle. You could have waited until he'd eaten, instead of announcing that in front of everyone!'

My father was furious. 'Go and see your husband.'

'He's OK . . . he's fine, he's crying on the bed.'

'I'm telling you, go and see your husband; go and see what's the matter with him!'

My mother added, 'Go and see him immediately. He hasn't eaten; he didn't even have a piece of bread! You're heartless!'

I went in there, grumbling. He was lying flat on his stomach, still sobbing loudly, 'Maman, my darling Maman. I'm going to lose you and I'm not even by your side, Maman.'

He was weeping about his mother's knee. It was a tragedy. I'd got it all wrong again. First, I should have told him after he'd eaten; and then, I should have done so in private, not at the table.

Crying like that over a knee . . . I was torn between uncontrollable nervous giggles and complete astonishment. What do you do when faced with an adult bawling like a baby?

Either he was play-acting or he was ill, but if he was, it was because of his mother.

'Maman, Maman.'

'Moussa, turn over, talk to me!'

I don't know how to be gentle and loving with adults. I wasn't taught how. I only know how to be like that with children, and he was really irritating me by sobbing so hard that he could no longer talk. I pulled him towards me, and saw that his face was distorted by tears. I gave up.

I walked out of the room, repeating incredulously, 'Bullshit. Bullshit . . . he's crying over his mother's knee! It's bullshit . . . '

My father banged on the table. 'You'll go and get the telephone and, even if it takes all night, you'll get hold of his mother and you'll pass her over to her son to earn his forgiveness. Understand?'

In the end, my mother-in-law had won. She wanted her son to call her back; she wanted money for the doctor, or she wanted him to come home to be coddled. Either way she had won.

Because Sunday evening calls are cheap rate and all Moroccans call each other at the same time, you need to be patient to get through. Either the lines are continually engaged, or for some unknown reason you get some Spanish operator or a friendly voice telling you to call back because the network is busy. After an hour I still couldn't get through. I had plonked myself on the floor with the telephone and I could still hear him blubbering, 'Maman, my darling Maman, I'm going to lose you.'

The last straw was that once I'd got through, when I asked his mother how she had been since that afternoon, her voice was positively sunny.

'I'm fine.'

'You're sure you're OK?'

'Yes! Yes! Never better . . . '

Thinking about it, since her husband had answered the phone first, I suppose she was having to talk in front of him, so there was more play-acting.

'I'm going to pass you over to your son.'

'Really?'

He didn't want to talk to her. 'No, I'm not well; I can't talk to her in this state.'

'Wait a moment, you've been crying for your mother for ages! Now she's on the phone, you're going to talk to her and you'll see it isn't anything serious. Hurry up because it's expensive!'

I heard everything.

'Hello, my son, my darling boy. I miss you. I don't know how I'm going to cope.'

She wanted him to come home. Now that he had obtained what he'd wanted, his papers, security in France, a working wife, she was keen to have him back. They both cried, but the knee wasn't even mentioned; my parents, who'd heard everything – I'd put the loudspeaker on – at least realised what a performance they were making.

What bad luck. I'd been landed with a possessive mother-in-law and a husband who had never grown up, and there was more to come.

He found an apprenticeship in the provinces. He'd come home on Friday evenings and leave again on Sunday. Things were going well. I decided we'd rent a studio flat to give my parents some space. He was earning 2,000 francs, but he was 'saving up' to buy a car. My own wages went on the rent and food and I couldn't even spend the rest; he did what he liked with it. I had to fight to furnish that flat; he didn't want to buy anything, not even a chest of drawers. He only wanted one thing, his car, so that he could run back to Morocco and show off.

My parents gave me everything: furniture, crockery, and a bed. The day I wanted to buy a sofa, he refused. In the end I'd had enough of this business with money. After all, I was earning virtually everything, so I took over the day-to-day running of the flat. We started quarrelling all the time.

My mother-in-law began to pester him. 'How come she still isn't pregnant?'

Then she sowed the seeds of doubt: perhaps I was secretly taking the pill?

So I was the one who didn't want children. To put an end to the argument, I announced that I'd made an appointment with a gynaecologist and that he would find out whether I could have children or not. Problem: although the gynaecologist was a Muslim, he was a man. I knew him; he'd already handed my parents two certificates of virginity, as well as a third just before the wedding. He was a doctor who knew me inside out, knew about my tetany attacks, my anorexia and my anxiety attacks from childhood. Moussa, however, didn't want a man examining me.

I said, 'It's him or no one!'

I trusted him completely, and told him, 'Habib, Moussa thinks I'm not fertile; you must do some tests on me.'

He burst out laughing. 'Fine, I'll do some tests for you, but what about him? Is he sure he's fertile?'

I had no problems. On the contrary, Habib said, joking about the scan, 'Run home quickly to see him! You're ovulating! If it still doesn't work, he's the one with a problem.'

Obviously, there was no way Moussa could have a problem. It still didn't happen, but he had a ready answer. 'It's because God doesn't want to give us a child for the time being.'

I wasn't in any hurry anyway, but eventually he decided to make an appointment, although his pride wouldn't let him tell me. He did in fact have a small problem that needed treatment, although he didn't discuss it with me. One day I accidentally chanced upon on a box of pills and I thought, 'Well, well! Is he taking medication then?'

'What's this?'

'Nothing. An intestinal problem.'

In fact, he had another problem, which had nothing to do with his intestines and which was temporarily stopping him from having children, but he wouldn't have admitted it for anything, not to me or his mother. It was much simpler to accuse me of infertility. I learned about it through my close relationship with the doctor. A few weeks of antibiotics and he could become a father. During this period my mother, cousins and friends questioned me constantly, telling me that if I didn't have a baby, my life would be ruined.

It was actually while I was telling one of the cousins that I wasn't in any great hurry to fall pregnant that I suddenly turned pale and was overcome by a feeling of nausea that sent me rushing to the bathroom. She watched me with a smile and came out with the traditional Arabic quip, 'Have you swallowed a fly?'

If I reviewed all the symptoms, it was entirely possible: feeling sleepy, bouts of sickness and other intimate details. However, I stubbornly continued making my wisecracks and rejecting the idea that I might be pregnant. No, not me, not now; I was too young; I had all the time in the world. I was actually hoping with all my heart that the miracle would happen. I would no longer be alone and unloved in the world.

The day I went to buy a test from the pharmacy, I was seething with excitement. I didn't even follow the instructions that recommended waiting until the next morning. I had to do it immediately. A thin pink line was supposed to appear on the stick I was holding reverently, as if it were sacred.

I waited there, sitting on my own in the bathroom, my

heart pounding. I finally saw a tiny line appear, but it was so faint and so thin that I wasn't sure I was seeing it properly. I stopped breathing to see more clearly, and then I ran over to the window to look at the test in daylight.

Eventually I rushed outside, ran through the neighbourhood, bumped into my friend Souria, who first thought I was mad, and then began running with me to the pharmacist, screaming with laughter. I didn't dare ask him what he thought, especially as he was so surprised to see me back so quickly that he thought I'd bungled the test.

Souria, who couldn't contain herself any longer, pushed me. 'Go on, show him!'

'But there are people around!'

'Who cares! You're married! Go on, show him! Monsieur, please can you tell us if this means she's pregnant?'

He said, 'Yes, probably,' and something inexplicable washed over me from head to toe. A completely unfamiliar sensation: happiness. It was the most wonderful day of my life.

When a blood test confirmed the news, I sat down on the laboratory steps, crying. I said, 'Thank you, thank you, Lord, for this happiness!' I floated through the town centre like a dragonfly, as if I were walking on air; I had my head in the clouds; nothing else existed. I had never experienced such a feeling of inebriation. I felt my stomach, I talked to this child who was still nothing and yet was everything to me.

'I'm finally going to be all right, because there are two of us now. You and me.'

I went to see my parents with my precious gift.

'How do you feel about having a grandson or a grand-daughter?'

They were happy, proud; my brothers and little sister had

been waiting for this child as impatiently as I had. Moussa was also proud; sure that he would have a son. We even argued in the nicest possible way about names; he wanted Mohammed, I wanted Ryad. Finally he let me have my own way. At that precise moment, the tranquillity I had spent so long hoping for was in reach. I was married, pregnant and everyone shared my happiness – my brothers, my sister, my parents and my husband. Finally I had a real life of my own; it belonged to me. If it was a girl she'd never go through what I had gone through. I promised myself that. If it was a boy I'd do everything in my power to make sure he wasn't brought up to be a male chauvinist: a French North African with the mentality of a guard dog.

I treasured the little test, like a photo depicting the first true happiness of my life. A tiny, pink line, a child like a light at the end of a tunnel. I was sure I'd be reborn at last along with my child.

CHAPTER EIGHT

Private life

'A DAUGHTER-IN-LAW WAITS ON her mother-in-law. She gets up before her, makes her something to eat, washes her dirty clothes, does her housework, runs her errands and gives her a bath.'

These, in a nutshell, were Moussa's mother's basic commands. She had come to 'help' with the birth of her grandson and was taking up all the space in our little flat. She completely disregarded the fact that I was having a baby and was worn out and jumpy due to a difficult, sleepless pregnancy. Every day, there was a problem.

'You know, son, I'm a guest and she didn't even get out of bed to make breakfast!'

I hadn't invited her. Her son had foisted her on me. She was sleeping in the lounge and I was finding it very hard not to bump into her unless I stayed in the bedroom or kitchen.

She was disturbed by the ticking of the clock, so we had to take it out every evening and shut it in a cupboard for the night, and then put it back in the morning. She couldn't bear the light from the street lamps: we had to keep the shutters closed and I had to hang a double curtain in the kitchen. She didn't move from the lounge; she just kept a close eye on everything I did and criticised it. I found the compulsory bathing ritual particularly difficult. She thought I was washing her badly and that I was doing it on purpose.

On the first day she'd asked me to lend her my hairbrush and some other personal toiletry items, claiming that she hadn't had time (in a month) to prepare for her trip. Thinking it would make her happy, I went out and bought her a complete set of toiletries: brush, comb, shampoo, shower gel, etc. She took the bag, looked me up and down, and put it down scornfully, as if I'd just humiliated her, saying to her son, 'Who does your wife think I am? I asked for *her* hairbrush and she didn't want to lend it to me! Why? What does she think? That I'm going to put a spell on her?'

It hadn't occurred to me, but why not . . .

I was completely bewildered by this strange mixture of demands. The woman was the personification of spite; she wanted me to be a docile, silent slave, calling on her son to witness my inability to wait on her, referring to a so-called tradition that I naturally rejected.

She had brought what was supposed to be a gift for me and the baby – a type of black *gandura*. At the wedding my sister-in-law had arrived dressed in black from head to toe. However, in our community black isn't worn for happy events. Wearing black or giving it as a gift is tantamount to wishing someone ill.

I couldn't sleep at night any more. Three weeks before I was due, the baby was too big and my cervix was closed, as if I were refusing to give birth and let my baby go. The doctor was concerned and I had to undergo a painful procedure to open my cervix. The contractions were terrible. I didn't want to see Moussa or his mother; I just wanted my family by my side. I felt as if I were about to have a tetany attack, closed in on myself, huddled up as I had in the bad days, and my mother knew how to massage me to make me feel better.

They wanted me to have the chance to give birth naturally and that was what I wanted, but when the anaesthetist arrived for the epidural, I thanked God. Moussa, who was waiting in the corridor of the clinic, took advantage of that to leave. 'My mother has been all on her own since you were brought in here. I can't leave her all on her own!'

I was shattered by this. If he'd have said, 'I'm tired. I'm going to have a rest and then I'll come back,' I would have understood. The real break with him occurred then.

The baby started to have breathing difficulties and my temperature was over 104° so they decided to give me an emergency Caesarean. I lost consciousness and Ryad was born, but his father was the last person to see him.

I was ashamed. My son's father had preferred to look after his mother. Then no one could find him. It was impossible to contact him to tell him about the birth and nothing was going as I'd planned. They had taken Ryad away to put him in an incubator for four days. I only had a photo and couldn't convince myself that this scrap of paper was really my son. It was unreal. I wasn't producing any milk yet. The first thing he knew was a rubber teat. I felt so unhappy, so empty . . . He was no longer in my belly. I could no longer talk to him as I'd done throughout my pregnancy. He no longer really belonged to me. He'd been taken from me.

When the family doctor came to see me, I dissolved into tears as I told him how depressed I felt.

The first day, my mother-in-law had sulked because my parents had arrived before her. She felt that it was her right to lord it over everyone by herself. Ryad was her grandson, not theirs. Since then Moussa had made a flying visit to see his son: she had forbidden him to leave her alone to see us. 'You understand, she waited for me yesterday. I stayed away too long; she hadn't eaten and she fainted.'

The insinuation was that it was because of me. When she came with him, it was to reduce me to tears with other insinuations before leaving again, taking her spiteful remarks with her. 'You couldn't even give birth normally! How did you come to give birth by Caesarean? You're not normal!'

She picked Ryad up. 'He looks like a drunkard . . . he doesn't even open his eyes.'

She never said his name. He was 'he'.

'Here, take this, buy him a little something.'

She had given me a 100-franc note, and then Moussa had stepped in. 'Give me back the 100 francs. You shouldn't have accepted it. I gave it to my mother.'

By my reckoning, those 100 francs had come out of my pocket anyway, because I was feeding the family. As a result, Moussa had given the money to his mother to give to me but, according to etiquette, I should have refused. It's not done to accept money from your mother-in-law. So the money had travelled from my account to Moussa, from Moussa to his mother and from his mother to me. I was supposed to say, 'Thank you, that's very kind of you,' and send it back in the opposite direction to my mother-in-law. It was stupid and nightmarish. I even had the occasional attack of the giggles, even if I did pay cash for them. Moussa hadn't even brought me a rose.

The day she saw one of my college friends arrive at the clinic, a trendy girl from Casablanca wearing a mini skirt and high heels, sporting short hair with blonde highlights, and holding a large bunch of flowers, some perfume and a bundle of baby clothes, I thought she was going to choke. Sadia had rushed over to the cradle. 'So you've produced this little miracle, have you? Isn't he handsome? Isn't he gorgeous!'

My mother-in-law immediately started interrogating her. 'Where do you come from? Are your parents Moroccan? Do you live in France? Where did you meet Leila? Do you work? Where do you live? Are you married? Oh, so you're not married . . . .'

Sadia replied, but I sensed she was feeling uncomfortable. We tried to talk in French, but my mother-in-law wrinkled her nose more and more.

When I was back home with my stomach stitched up, she was no more solicitous. She even said to me, 'I'm your mother now! You don't belong to your family any more; you belong to our family.'

When I left the clinic, she'd ordered me to move in with my parents so that she could be alone with her son. 'You can go back to your parents' place; don't come back to my son's flat or else who'll look after you and your son?'

She certainly wouldn't. I was in a bad physical condition, and Ryad wasn't sleeping through the night and was crying constantly; so was I. They'd kept me in the clinic for a fortnight and I was still not up and about.

The doctor, who knew my situation inside out, mother-in-law included, had summoned Moussa. 'Your wife is depressed. She has stopped eating and isn't sleeping; I'm warning you, if she has to come back to hospital for some reason, you'll have me to reckon with. Make sure she gets some peace and quiet and that she and the baby have everything they need.'

Also, between Moroccans, he dared to quip in Arabic. 'Is it true that people are very money-conscious in your region?'

Moussa had been affronted by this joke. 'Who does that stupid bastard think he is?'

The doctor had given me some medication and had sent a psychologist to see me before I was discharged, but I'd begun crying, unable to say anything but 'I can't stand it any more.'

So I was supposed to go to my parents on the orders of my mother-in-law, but my mother advised me against it. 'Leila, don't do that; she'll criticise you for it tomorrow and the day after tomorrow and for the rest of your life.'

'But why? She's the one who told me to!'

'A mother-in-law always tells her daughter-in-law the opposite of what she wants.'

It was a question of etiquette, some kind of test . . . I found it hard to understand, possibly because of omissions in my overly Westernised upbringing. I went home unwillingly. Besides, it didn't feel like home. I felt as if I were descending into hell.

'Why didn't you go back to your parents like I told you to?'

'My parents live too far away, there isn't a pharmacy there and there's a pharmacy downstairs here.'

An answer in line with accepted etiquette, suggested by Maman.

Ryad wasn't sleeping through the night, but he was a real glutton, needing a bottle every two hours. Moussa slept. His mother snored. I was getting up every hour and a half. I'd tiptoe across the lounge in the dark. I'd shut the kitchen door so that the light didn't disturb the snoring woman, and I'd make up the bottle while Ryad bawled. So my mother-in-law grumbled and Moussa continued sleeping.

I couldn't see to my son and make up his bottle at the same time. My stitches pulled too much to carry him and a saucepan at the same time. I also had to remember to remove that wretched clock every evening, close the shutters, get up early for breakfast, prepare the meal and give my mother-in-law her bath. At home, another daughter-in-law washed her. She could have done it perfectly well herself, but that was out of the question. The rule: your mother-in-law is here, she's getting on in years, and so you wash her back. No point in buying a brush so that she could manage on her own. Moussa would have thrown it in my face.

I sensed that he was changing. I could no longer communicate with him. He wasn't working and he suddenly started saying his prayers assiduously and reading the Koran. I'm a believer; I observe Ramadan, but I'm not excessively religious. Nor are my parents. Moussa was now discussing religion with his mother all the time; he even owned some cassette tapes of the Koran and they prayed together. I don't know what was going through his head to alter his behaviour like this. I can still see both of them crouching in the lounge. Me sitting in a chair, worn out, her pleased, saying, 'My dear son, you've come back to religion, that's good.'

I couldn't even watch television any more. She criticised me for not having a satellite dish for the Arabic channels. Changing Ryad was another source of conflict. The changing table was in the lounge. I didn't have anywhere else to put it until we had a larger flat, and my mother-in-law couldn't bear to see the nappies. 'That stinks, take those nappies to the bin downstairs!'

We were three floors up, so every time I changed my son, I was forced to go downstairs to throw *one* nappy into the rubbish chute. There was a bin in the flat and sealed bags, but it wasn't enough; it couldn't wait until the evening, I had to take them down one by one.

She hardly ever held Ryad. And the few times she did, he screamed.

Once, she had decided to make the meal. That was when I became anorexic.

'Leila, come and eat.'

'No, thank you, I don't feel very well, I'm not hungry.'

In the evening, Moussa asked his mother to make something to eat.

'Oh no, I'm not setting foot in that kitchen again. Your wife doesn't trust me; she's afraid that I'm putting a curse on her.'

'That's not true. She told me she wasn't hungry.'

'No, she didn't eat what I made this lunchtime; it's because she doesn't trust me, so I'm not lifting a finger now.'

She was clearly trying to come between us in order to get her son back. Now he had his papers, he no longer needed me.

'Son, the baby is crying all the time and I'm afraid all on my own in this lounge. Come and sleep with me and leave the baby with your wife. That way you'll get some decent sleep, my dear son.'

He did as she said. He got into the habit of sleeping with his mother in the lounge. At the age of 35! He used a weird argument to justify himself: 'I sleep with my mother because when she leaves, I'll no longer have a mother, so I'm making the most of every moment.'

She had completely isolated me. The arguments became more acrimonious. I said what I had to say to my husband, despite my mother-in-law, but without involving her. She pushed me to the limit so often that, unsurprisingly, the situation eventually came to a head. I think that was what she was angling for, in order to crush me once and for all in her son's eyes.

She had again asked me to give her a bath, a chore that was made even more difficult by the fact that my stomach still hurt and my scar was ugly and inflamed. I washed her shoulders and back in silence.

'Wash lower down!'

This was asking too much. I have never washed an adult's backside. Babies, my little brothers, sure. But an elderly mother-in-law weighing 180 pounds, no way.

'I can't bend down any lower. My stomach hurts too much.'

I quietly walked out of the bathroom. I had been polite. She got out of the bath and stormed into the lounge, screaming to her son who merely watched the skirmish in silence.

'Your wife didn't want to wash me!'

'Of course I did . . . I did what I had to do.'

'You didn't want to!'

'I can't bend any lower; it isn't that I don't *want* to, I *can't*. If you don't believe me, look at my scar!'

I showed her the size of the scar that was still suppurating, so she'd understand once and for all that my refusal wasn't personal. However, I was speaking logically and acting logically, which was alien to my mother-in-law. What had I done just then? I had made an obscene gesture in front of my mother-in-law. I had shown her my stomach.

Moussa had gone out, leaving us to fight. He was sick and

tired of it, which I could understand, but he was fortunate to be able to leave and not hear his mother screaming. I was trapped and I couldn't stand it any longer because of my tiredness, my lack of sleep and my weakness; she was putting me on edge. I took refuge in my bedroom and, having gone way beyond etiquette, I slammed the door, saying, 'Shit, I'm sick and tired of this!'

When her son came back, she started screaming and crying, making an incredible song and dance. 'I'm not staying here, because your wife doesn't look after me. I didn't come almost 2,000 miles to be humiliated like this; I'm not here to be treated like a dog; you don't realise, son! She shows me no respect, she pulled down her trousers, she showed me her backside, she called me "a pain in the arse".'

I tried to set things straight with Moussa. I had shown her my stomach, not my backside. I'd said 'shit'; I hadn't called her a 'pain in the arse' – and anyway, it was out of the question for me to wash his mother's backside. Also, while we were on the subject, she would do well to fill the bathtub once when she had a bath, not five times in a row, because hot water is expensive. She'd climb into the water, soak in it like a hippopotamus, empty the bathtub, fill it up again and start over, four or five times in a row, just for pleasure. But I was the one paying the bill, and anyway, she was going to wear me down in the end, I just knew it. I was stuck in a living hell instead of enjoying being with my son. She was doing her son's head in, trying to make him admit that I was a bad girl.

'Your wife doesn't listen, your wife gets it into her head to do something and she does it; you're her husband, she must tell you where she's going, she mustn't wear trousers, she mustn't go out on her own.'

So Moussa started to ask me, 'Where were you? Where are you going? What are you doing?'

I'd put up with enough hassle in my life and I wasn't going to have this type of thing start all over again with him. Eventually, I spoke my mind. 'All right, then, sod it, if you're not happy, clear out and take your mother with you, that would suit me down to the ground! I've got a job, a flat and a son, and I don't need you! After all, what have you ever done for me?'

'What have I done for you? I've made you respectable: I've "covered your head"! You're married!'

'Anyway, I've never loved you and I never will.'

'Oh yes? Oh yes? So why did you have a child with me?'

'You're the one who had a child with me! But Ryad is here and he's my son. I carried him! Not you! Now you have to choose, it's her or me!'

I felt as if the physical and nervous anxiety that I'd experienced before and had almost driven me mad was threatening to sweep over me again and I was afraid. I had to protect my son now; I had to be strong for him. But my mother-in-law didn't let the matter drop. She screamed I was being rude to her son, and then she even came into my bedroom and stood between us, yelling that she wouldn't allow me to speak to my husband in that way. I told her where to get off.

'This is none of your business. This is between my husband and me.'

'Don't talk to my mother like that! I'm going to call your father and we'll talk about this later.'

'Call who you want, I don't give a damn!'

I was 23 and it was starting all over again as before, as always. If that cantankerous woman hadn't meddled in our married life, I think we might have been able to live together normally. In my husband's defence, the failure of our marriage was entirely due to his mother. He was conforming to North African tradition by allowing her to stay in our flat, a prisoner of the etiquette that gives the mother-in-law a central role to play in the birth of the first child. He granted her exclusive rights because he had been conditioned to do so and had never known any different. I was furious to see him being so weak, when I should have felt sorry for him.

This time, my mother-in-law and my father sat in judgement on me. 'Your daughter is badly brought up. She's rude to her husband.'

My father didn't say anything. He must've realised that I was at the end of my tether and he didn't like the woman either. He had married me off by force and my mother-in-law had been imposed on me. I was still waiting for a gesture, a word from him.

'Leila, is it true what your mother-in-law is saying?'

I told him about everything, trying to remain calm, but I couldn't do it. My father took me to one side. 'She isn't here for long. You must learn to control yourself. Do it for Ryad. Not for her or for me, but for your son.'

He left, saying to Moussa and his mother, 'I apologise for her!'

But not me. There was no way I was going to apologise. He'd barely left the flat when she attacked me again. 'Now take that nappy downstairs!'

'No! There's a bin here. In France, this is what happens. I'll take down the rubbish bag when it's full.'

She squatted down, her legs tucked under her, and put on a show that staggered me. 'I've fallen over! She's going to drive me crazy! She's going to drive me crazy.'

And she kept screaming endlessly. She scratched her face. She took off her headscarf to curse me. 'Leila, one for me, ten for you!'

In other words, if one curse befalls me, ten will befall you. I looked at this spectacle, thinking, 'My God, I can't believe it, this isn't really happening, I'm caught in a nightmare.'

I was in the process of changing Ryad on the changing table in the lounge when this unbelievable scene suddenly started. I stood there, a nappy in my hand, my baby lying there waiting, unable to move. Moussa suddenly appeared out of nowhere and, seeing his mother in that state, also threw a fit of hysterics.

He ripped his shirt, beat his chest and scratched himself until he drew blood: he was totally hysterical. 'I'll never forgive you. You've hurt my mother. You want to kill my mother.'

I looked at them both, that elderly woman and that adult man, wide-eyed with amazement.

She stood up and pushed me violently against the wall. 'I'll never forgive you! You've taken my son away from me! I swear on the Koran that you won't remain my son's wife. You don't deserve him!'

I saw red in my turn; this hysteria was bound to be contagious in the long run. 'I took your son? Who's taken whose life? Who came to ask for whose hand in marriage? Who didn't want to get married? Who didn't want anything to do with him? I detest you! I hate you both! I never wanted this man. He's mad; we have nothing in common. You think your son is so wonderful, you think he's irreplaceable? There are much better men than him and I deserve better than him! He's the one who doesn't deserve me.'

I could even have said that he had merely used me to obtain his papers, but I wasn't even thinking of that any more. I was beside myself with rage. That expression: 'You don't deserve my son' had been too hard to bear, unsurprisingly.

I insulted Moussa. 'You stupid bastard! You've taken everything from me, you've taken everything from me!'

They had driven me crazy. I couldn't see straight any more. I left the flat in socks and a T-shirt, pelted down the stairs and ran outside in midwinter. It was snowing and I had only one thought, to top myself. If there'd been a balcony, I would have leaped into thin air. I ran through the entire neighbourhood in a fury, and threw myself into a phone box and called my mother.

'You know what, Maman? Everyone can sod off; they can all go to hell! You've lost your daughter; you've lost her for ever. Goodbye! Look after Ryad, that's all I ask of you.'

Even Ryad didn't exist for me any more at that time. I crossed that urban development area at a run; I wanted to die. I was racing towards the main road, saying to myself, 'Go on, just kill yourself once and for all.' I wanted a lorry to appear and run me over.

Strangely, I always met someone at the very last minute when I hit rock bottom. A car drew up driven by a friend of the family, Juliette – a tall, good-hearted 'mamma' who had jet-black skin and a forceful, generous nature. She had recognised me shivering by the roadside, my face covered in blood after hitting my head in the phone box.

'Leila? What are you doing here? What's happened to you?'

I was sobbing. I couldn't speak. The words remained stuck in my head. I felt as if I had suddenly been struck dumb and that I'd never be able to talk again. She tried to make me climb into her car, but I was struggling in a suffocating silence. I didn't want anything to do with her or her car. I wanted to throw myself under the wheels of a lorry. I wanted it to flatten me and my shitty life.

She realised I was really in danger.

'You're going to get into this car or else. If I have to slap you, I'll slap you! Get in!'

As I pushed her away, she caught hold of me by the neck and lifted me like a feather. I was so thin and she was so strong that it wasn't difficult for her. She fastened the belt around me in the back seat. 'Don't move! I'm taking you back to my place!'

She put me in her bedroom and when I could utter a word, I stammered, begging her: 'No one . . . don't tell . . . alone . . . alone . . . '

I wanted to be totally alone, I was lost, in a panic; my brain wasn't working any more.

'OK, I'll leave you here on your own, but I'm locking you in! Listen carefully; I'll be next door. I'm not going anywhere. Cry your heart out, scream if you want, but even if you have to spend all day here, you're not moving until you can speak properly and think clearly.'

She locked me in. I huddled up in the armchair and really cried. I stared into space. I couldn't get my breath from time to time; the sobs were catching in my throat. I now wonder where all those tears came from.

During this time my mother had alerted all her friends and had sent my brothers to find me. They were doing the rounds of the blocks of flats. One of them rang Juliette's door.

'No, I haven't seen Leila. Why? What's happened?'

'My sister has gone missing . . . if you see her, you must tell us . . . '

Juliette wanted to tell him that I was there, but she didn't know what had happened, and above all she didn't know who had put me in such a state. She thought I was running away; that was serious, but she still hadn't realised that I wanted to throw myself under a lorry, since I hadn't even been able to tell her.

I stayed at her place for the rest of the day. Once I had cried myself dry, my brain gradually regained its faculties. I couldn't stand this life, but other girls who had been married by force like me put up with it. I knew some of them. I thought they were spoiling their chances of living here and being free in a free country. I thought I was pathetic, passing from fits of despair to frantic getaways, from tetany attacks to suicidal depression. I never stopped struggling and fighting, but I never won. All the people who used to talk about integration could never rescue us: they didn't have all the necessary information. Even we girls from the schools and colleges would get hit up, claiming that our parents would 'never' do that to us. They'd never marry us by force to some North African immigrant, because we'd say 'no'. However, in most cases we were forced to say 'yes'. We were caught in a system. Some of these women had children, and I had the impression that they were going to make their daughters suffer the same thing. Endlessly repeating their own experiences. Where was the answer? The Muslim community in France hadn't made any headway since I was born – it had been going backwards. At school I had never seen girls wearing headscarves, and now you see them parading through the streets.

What can be done to make families adapt and evolve? Should there be a designated area where they could exert their authority as they wish, keeping girls behind closed doors? Certainly not, since this enclosed area already exists in certain neighbourhoods. The only place these girls can breathe freely is at school and college, while acquiring an education. Knowledge is what allows them to transcend antiquated traditions and to develop – a place where everyone's religion and traditions can be left at the door.

When I watch reports about the girls who want to wear headscarves at school because it's their choice, I really have my doubts. Some of them may do it to regain a lost identity, a teenage crisis that takes a different form from mine. However, I know many of the girls wear veils just for some peace and quiet, so that their brothers will leave them alone. 'My sister wears a headscarf, it's good, I can rest easy!'

One such girl told me, 'Between you and me, since I've been wearing a headscarf, my brothers, parents and everyone else leave me alone. I can go where I want and do what I like. I have boyfriends and I can smoke a fag in peace, since they'd never imagine that I might smoke a cigarette because I'm wearing a headscarf!'

I'm not at all keen on that solution, for a start because it's still based on a lie, and also because the headscarf can insidiously encourage parents, brothers and husbands to become more and more deeply steeped in religion: no one is safe. Almost overnight, we can come face to face with hardline fundamentalism. Moussa was in the process of doing just that.

Moreover, if they made wearing the headscarf legal in France, it wouldn't be possible to prevent families from imposing it on their daughters. 'Since you're allowed to wear it at school, you must wear it!' Already, some girls are being forced by their parents to wear the headscarf so that it's easier to marry them off, because there are men who want this.

As for me, I hadn't moved on. Trapped between my husband and my mother-in-law, I was moving forward at a crawl, like an ant. It was like being a teenager all over again. Every time I managed to make my parents or someone like Moussa understand something, the ant took a step forward.

This time the ant had almost been crushed underfoot. I'd behaved like a head case. I had left my son on his own – I'd left my little baby with those two hysterics! And to do what? To kill myself and leave him alone for ever! I deserved a good slapping.

Juliette allowed my kid brother to come in when he rang the doorbell again. He was crying into the intercom. Maman had collected Ryad, whom my mother-in-law had plonked on the doormat in his Moses basket. Barely had she half-opened my front door when she launched a furious attack on my mother. 'So you've come to defend your daughter, have you? Do you have any idea what your daughter has done?'

She told her about my refusal to wash her backside and the way I had indecently showed her my stomach. As far as my mother was concerned, the problem was simple. 'Leave them be. My daughter has done everything she can to ensure things go smoothly with Moussa and then you turn up and ruin their life. My daughter isn't in the way here – this is her home – but if she has to come home to us, she'll come with her son.'

As for Moussa, he really got it in the neck. 'And you, I'm warning you! You'll know all about it if anything happens to my daughter or my grandson.'

I think she would have been capable of persuading my father to begin legal proceedings against him in Morocco. He was starting to feel afraid and he suggested that he go looking for me. She sent him about his business. If anyone was going to bring me back, it would be her, not him. And she took the baby with her.

My mother-in-law started yelling again. 'You're a woman and you're telling your family what to do, are you?'

'Isn't that what you're trying to do?'

When, later on, my mother described this battle of the mothers-in-law with Moussa stuck in the middle, I felt temporarily avenged for my unhappiness. They confronted each other in all earnestness, a proper Arab-style battle, trading insults as they would have done back in the village. And finished up with, 'Do you think your son Moussa is a man? He sleeps with his mother instead of his wife. Is that normal?'

'Aiouili . . . She's speaking about my son's sexuality!'

Then the 'mummy's boy' launched himself into the battle for his honour. 'What makes my sexuality any business of yours? Who took your daughter? Who covered her head? Who has stopped people from talking about her?'

'The worse mistake we ever made, and I'll regret it for the rest of my life, is having given our daughter to you!'

Meeting adjourned. Mother and son had a fresh attack of hysterics.

'Darling Maman, I brought you over here, forgive me; may God forgive me because I'm making you suffer, I'm making you cry.'

My mother told me she had felt as if she were in a film.

So I went back to my parents' flat with Ryad. Back to safety. I'd already secretly been thinking about divorce while I was carrying my son, but I kept that idea to myself for the time being. I couldn't spend my life with that man and let him raise my child. He was barely a month old and he had already heard lunatics screaming around him. Neither he nor I would be able to lead a normal life.

My father was beginning to understand and had said to

me, 'You're not going back home while that other woman is still there.'

I was furious, all the same. I was the one paying the rent. I hadn't saved a penny and, if anything were to happen to Ryad, I wouldn't know what to do.

The days went by and every morning my father would take me home so that the nurse could give me my injection to prevent phlebitis. She made home visits and I couldn't ask her to travel even further afield. My father waited for me in the car.

'Above all, don't make a scene.'

I'd go in and watch them sleeping, still together, unaware that the day had begun and that people were working around them. So I'd make a noise. I'd slam doors and drawers and I'd even put on some music.

'That's enough, Leila! Stop making such a noise, my mother's sleeping!'

'I don't care. I'm looking for something.'

I still didn't tell them that this was my home. The time hadn't yet come. First, I wanted his mother to return to Morocco, with him, if possible.

One morning I decided to provoke them. I arrived wearing make-up, with my hair done and dressed as if I were going on a date. Normally I looked pretty terrible, incapable of taking the slightest interest in my appearance. I was hoping they'd give up when confronted by what they considered as an intolerable attack and get out of my home.

Moussa walked into the trap. 'Where are you going dressed like that?'

'Suddenly you're interested in what I'm doing? That's new.'

'You're wearing make-up, you're all dressed up and you haven't got Ryad with you: where are you going?'

'That's absolutely none of your business. Bye, see you tomorrow.'

On another day his mother woke up, and as soon as she saw me, covered her head with the blanket. I let rip in French. 'Get out, you vicious woman . . . you fool! That woman is really so stupid! Do you really think I didn't see you hiding!'

I knew she was going to complain to her son. 'She insulted me in French; I didn't understand.' But as he was sleeping, he couldn't translate for her. They slept all the time. All they did was discuss the Koran, pray, eat and sleep – but they were doing it in my home, and he was feeding his mother at my expense. She had wanted fish, so there was fish in the kitchen, whereas once, one wretched time during my pregnancy, I'd had a terrible craving for fish and he'd replied, 'It's too expensive!'

I had really insulted him that morning.

'Moussa, you bastard! Fish was too expensive for me, was it? So what about the fish you're stuffing into your face now? Who paid for that?'

'Why are you insulting me?'

'What about the car you drive your mother around in? Who bought that? Nothing's too expensive for your mother when I'm shelling out for it, is it?'

She obviously wanted to take advantage of this scene. 'She's impossible! You can't keep her, son! You'll be unhappy. Look how she acts with just with one child. Don't have any more children, son, don't have any more children!'

I still had to be the one who wanted more children with her son. I left the flat, slamming the door.

After two weeks I was fed up with all this coming and going and not having my things – and of provoking them without any real results. I gave it some thought: 'Leila, you work, you're on maternity leave, but you still have your wages and they're taking advantage of them – and, when it comes down to it, she's won because you left. If you continue to stay with your parents, she'll never leave. She'll stay put in your flat with her beloved son and you'll be left with nothing. So you need a change of tactics, my girl; you're going home!'

This was war. I had just decided to kill my marriage in cold blood.

CHAPTER NINE

Premeditated murder

I RACED THROUGH THE final chapters of my diary, which has remained secret until now, as if I were running one last marathon. I was out of breath as I crossed the finishing line.

I wasn't a heroine or a fighter. I often compared myself to a poor trapped fly forbidden to take to the air; or, occasionally, to an ant slowly and cautiously making its way through dangerous territory. My mother-in-law was poisoning my existence as a wife and mother and I wanted her out of my life. She was taking away my only source of happiness: my son. The hateful behaviour of that 65-year-old woman, who was so unhealthily attached to her 35-year-old son that she slept with him and constantly brainwashed him, caused Moussa and me to fight all the time. She was destroying his life and he was just as trapped as I was.

I had gone back to work. I was coping in the conjugal home, inasmuch as Ryad was with my mother. I needed a social security document, though, so I went to the town hall to obtain it. The employee behind the desk said to me, 'Tell your husband that we are still missing various documents needed to complete his mother's file.'

'What file?'

'The application for a residence permit!'

'I didn't know anything about this!'

That was how I discovered that my husband had brought in my payslips, and an affidavit allegedly signed by me and by him, saying that we were happy to take responsibility for his mother. He had described her as a 'widow with no means of support'. On the one hand, I hadn't signed any document – he had forged my signature – and on the other, my father-in-law wasn't dead and, what's more, was wealthy enough to provide for his wife's needs. If he had no longer been able to do so, his sons were more than capable of doing so in Morocco, but I certainly couldn't on the pittance I earned.

Moussa had produced a forged death certificate for his own father, which the employee was now examining from every angle.

'How did he get hold of this?'

'I don't know, but you can have anything made on demand.'

'Really. So that's the way it is, eh? I'll take care of them.'

'I'd rather they didn't know that I was involved. My situation is complicated enough with them.'

'Don't worry, it's very simple. I'll ask him for the family record book; deaths are usually recorded in that.'

Of course, Moussa was unable to provide the relevant family record book with an entry for the deceased. He was furious, but cornered, and he never knew how. My mother-in-law had to kiss her residence permit goodbye, as well as the basic old-age pension and the free social security benefits, with a small fortune in Morocco standing by, just in case.

Her scheme might have worked. There are many others. In Morocco go-betweens offer money to girls there on holiday to 'make papers'. 'I'll give you any sum of money you want, he won't lay a finger on you, you won't lay a finger on him, and you will take him back to France.'

Families have brought children into France who weren't theirs – even newborn babies. I suppose they register them first in Morocco under their surname, like children born out of wedlock, and there you have it, they'll be raised in France. Others are worse: they bring over young girls bearing their surname to be used as maidservants. I've known some who ran away in the end because they were so badly treated. Virtually everyone has heard their stories around the neighbourhood.

It makes me sick to talk about it, but you can buy any type of document in our community – a birth or death certificate or a certificate of celibacy. I knew of one case of a married man who paid a young French woman of North African origin so that he could marry her with a forged certificate of celibacy. Because the Moroccan marriage certificate isn't recognised in France, no enquiries were made beforehand. Once he had obtained his identity papers, the man divorced his wife in France and brought his real wife and daughter into the country. The system is simple: he divorced his real wife, and then remarried her at the consulate according to the correct procedures. These things are known and talked about, but no one denounces them. You'd need to have the mind of an informer.

This type of scheme particularly infuriates me because its success relies on marrying off girls. Whether these girls are Moroccan, French with North African immigrant parents or wholly French, they are victims. The illegal immigrants say that it's easier to target a French girl. For a start, it's cheaper. You don't have to worry about a dowry or spend a king's ransom on the wedding.

Playing the bashful lover is very easy. They're good at that; they turn on the charm and the girl believes them, whereas the boy is using her and her feelings to get what he wants. Who ends up in pieces? She does. Either she's taken back to the North African village or she's pushed to breaking point until she asks for a divorce. One of my friends fell into such a trap. I tried everything to make her understand.

'Sylvie, think about it; you've only known him for two months, he stopped you in the street, you only see him in cafés, he's an illegal immigrant!'

'No! He's a student; he's studying to be an engineer! He has a residence permit!'

Everyone knows about the students who are studying to be engineers. Either their residence permit is forged or they are actually students, but their permit is running out. That was the case with this boy. He was tall, handsome and slender, all smiles, and the girl wasn't particularly attractive. Her family was worried, especially her brother, because she was obviously being conned.

'He's the love of my life, Leila; my parents don't understand. It was love at first sight for him and he wants us to get married.'

I lost my temper. 'A complete stranger picks you up in the street in the middle of Paris; he invites you for a coffee, he turns your head when you're only waiting for one thing: someone to fall in love with you. I swear, on my son's life, that he'll ask you to marry him before his residence permit runs out.'

'That's not true.'

'Yes, it is! That guy spotted you, and realised you were dreaming of a great love! If you marry him, he'll obtain his identity papers double quick, and then do a runner or take you back to North Africa and make your life hell until you ask for a divorce.'

'That's not true; you shouldn't generalise just because you've had a bad experience.'

The French think in French, not Arabic; but as a French-born girl of North African immigrant parents, I think in both languages. As I'd predicted my friend's romance resulted in marriage before his residence permit expired. He had also promised her a lavish wedding in Algeria: she's still waiting. She hardly ever talked about love after that. However, no one had forced her. Her parents love her and she hadn't lived the life I had; she just wanted to be loved, like everybody does.

In my case I'd decided to kill off my marriage with no other weapon than my rotten temper, which probably came from my Berber origins. One particular thing made me hopping mad: the car that Moussa had bought with my money, for which I was responsible because the registration documents were in my name and so was the insurance. He would even ask me to fill it up for him so he could collect Ryad, whom my parents had been babysitting during the day since I'd gone back to work. I was afraid to leave my son alone with his father. He didn't keep an eye on him, and would leave him alone in the flat to go out for a coffee when he was only three months old.

This business with the car provoked the first act of physical violence. I was actually the one who started it. I couldn't bear seeing his mother lording it in my seat in the car and being ferried about like royalty while I had to walk everywhere. The row began as he was parking outside the block of flats. I watched his mother get out, my stomach knotted with rage. I waited until she had gone into the building and charged over to Moussa.

'Open the door!'

'I'm warning you, if you make a scene here . . . '

'I don't give a damn about a scene! Do you think it's normal that your mother has plonked herself in my flat and that she's being ferried about in *my* car?'

'It isn't your flat! It's our flat!'

'No! It's my flat!'

I went over the whole business again from scratch, from the very start, expressing myself with reckless violence and aggressiveness. I attacked him and his mother from every angle. I was even vulgar and he fell into the trap by attacking my mother.

'And what about your mother? Who does she think she is? She said I wasn't sleeping with my wife!'

'You sleep with your mother, don't you?'

'Then perhaps yours wants me to screw her!'

I slapped him: it was a knee-jerk reaction. He went white. 'Get out of this car immediately.'

'I'm not moving.'

'Get out of this car or else!'

'No. Whose name is on the registration documents? Mine! The insurance? Mine! So you can just shut up. If anyone should get out of the car, it's you!'

'Here, take your keys, take everything, I don't want anything to do with this car.'

'Thank you, that's all I wanted.'

He dashed off to join his beloved Maman. I took the car keys and phoned one of my brothers, who'd just passed his driving test.

'What's wrong now?'

'You passed your driving test, didn't you? Here, you've got a car now, you can drive.'

My father tried to calm me down. 'No, Leila! Don't go to those lengths.' But the look in his eyes said, 'I'm not meddling in any of this any more. I'm losing control.' My brother went off with the car, happy as anything.

Moussa wasn't expecting me to act so fast. 'Where's the car?'

'Gone! It's mine and I've just given it away. Stupid, eh?'

'Who's got it?'

'Forget it! There's nothing you can do about it! Are you going to go to the police station and lodge a complaint? It's mine and no one has stolen it from me!'

That evening, after collecting Ryad from my parents, I warned one of my neighbours, a French woman with whom I was particularly friendly. I said, 'I'm going home. If you hear any banging on the wall, don't worry; it's to be expected. War has been declared.'

'Do you want me to keep Ryad here with my son?'

'If there's a problem, I'll bring him over to you! I'm off. All's fair in love and war!'

I saw a mother-in-law glowing with happiness, flopped on the sofa, pleased to be alone with her beloved son and thinking that she had won. As soon as she noticed me, her smile faded and the mask dropped.

She stared at Moussa fixedly as if she were hypnotising him and telling him not to go near us. Suddenly he was incapable of taking his son in his arms in the face of that unspoken order.

She attacked first. 'What are you doing here? Why have you come?'

'Because I'll tell you something between the two of us: this is my home. OK? This is my flat.'

'You could have had enough respect to wait for me to leave.'

'Hold on a minute and I'll explain! You're going to pack your bags very soon and leave.'

'Don't speak to my mother like that!'

'You, come into the bedroom.'

I don't know why, but for some time I had been talking to him in the way my father talked. I felt strong, determined to win: she had to leave. He followed me without a word.

'Listen to me carefully. Are you wide awake? Are you listening very carefully?'

'Go on, what do you want?'

'Today's Wednesday. Your mother will be out of here by Saturday morning at the latest! I don't care how you manage it, just do it!'

'But how am I going to afford to pay for the ticket?'

'Oh, yes! That reminds me. I've switched accounts and my wages are no longer being paid into our joint account, so if you have any savings, you'd better use them.'

'Why did you do that!'

'Because all my wages were going into the joint account while all your money goes to Morocco. I don't see a penny of your unemployment benefits! So I've opened a personal account. It's over, Moussa! No more goose with the golden eggs!'

'We'll see about that.'

'There's nothing left to see!'

'What if we're still here on Saturday? What will you do then?'

'You're taking a big risk. Either you take her peacefully

back to Morocco and she's still alive, or you risk finding her sellotaped to the wall one day or hanging from the ceiling light. It's up to you, but I swear it, if she hasn't gone by Saturday, I'll smash her face in at the slightest remark.'

He looked at me oddly; I was frightening him, and he felt humiliated at having to convey the news to his mother. I suppose he claimed that it was all his decision; in any case, she didn't say anything. I did, however, hear a phone conversation with one of his brothers, who told him unequivocally, 'It's our mother who's messed up things between the two of you.'

His father had added, 'If I'd come to France, none of these problems would have happened. Your mother's a nasty piece of work. Wherever she goes she has to cause trouble.'

He didn't know that his son had killed him off on paper. Is that the type of behaviour they call Freudian?

I listened with delight; the phone's loudspeaker was always switched on when one of us called Morocco, so that the whole family could hear the news. My mother-in-law was extremely upset. 'Even my own son isn't on my side, even my own husband isn't on my side!'

She was the victim. On Friday morning, he announced that they were leaving. 'Tomorrow, I'm catching the coach with my mother. I'm taking her home to Morocco.'

'Fine. Have a good trip.'

I had used the enemy's weapons, Arabic-style: endless discussions, humiliation and insults; I had devised an unbeatable scheme and my mother, to whom I had told everything, was just as happy as I was. For once, she was my ally, but I still hadn't mentioned divorce . . .

I shall never forget the Friday I gained my freedom. My mother-in-law was in the kitchen making food to eat during the trip. I hadn't bought or prepared anything; Moussa had been forced to do the shopping himself. I thought, 'You can cope on your own now; these are the last hours you will ever spend in my kitchen!'

I didn't help her pack or do her washing or bathe her, which I strictly should have done. She washed herself unaided in the bathtub and I didn't fail to remind her that in France we only fill the bath once. 'You wash yourself, you rinse yourself and that's that.'

She didn't say anything then, but at the evening meal, she said, 'You know, Leila, you should make more of an effort with your husband. You don't belong to your father's family any more, you belong to Moussa's.'

'Listen carefully, I'm my father's daughter and my son is his grandson. He's the fruit of my womb and your son put him there; I have a father and a mother, just as he has a father and a mother.'

I went back into my bedroom, slamming the door. At 4 a.m. they were about to leave. I heard, 'Leila, get up! At least come and say goodbye.'

'Goodbye, and don't make any noise or you'll wake Ryad up. Lock the door on your way out, please.'

They left. I began to scream with joy like a kid. 'Waouhouh! I'm on holiday, at last!'

A peaceful fortnight passed. I felt at ease; nothing could get to me any more. My sister-in-law phoned me with an account of their return, pleased that I had in some way taken my revenge on the dragon. She called me again, and said, 'Leila, I promised to warn you: he's gone. He'll be back on Monday morning at dawn. Be careful.'

'Be careful about what? I've got nothing to feel guilty about.'

'He has a grudge against your family and I've never seen him so annoyed.'

I wasn't overly worried. On the other hand, I was furious that he hadn't asked after his son for two weeks. My little Ryad, my little ray of sunshine, hadn't known a trouble-free day without us fighting since he had been in my womb.

I prepared myself psychologically all weekend. My plan was diabolic. He would arrive home tired and would want to sleep, so while he was sleeping, I'd take his keys from his pocket and hide them. I'd lock the front door to the flat and we'd fight it out, just him and me behind closed doors. A duel. I was preparing myself for a fight to the death.

I'd warned my neighbours across the landing, still doing my clown routine. 'He's coming! I think the battle will last a few hours. You're going to hear some unpleasant stuff: if you hear me call for help, come to my rescue! If you hear him, stay put.'

I was laughing nervously, but I knew very well that this type of fight between husband and wife can take a tragic turn.

He arrived in the early hours of the morning, surprised to find me alone with Ryad. He was expecting me to be surrounded by my brothers for this battle.

I was pretending to sleep, but I was keeping watch. He took a shower and came to lie down next to me. I got up and went to lie down on the sofa with my son.

I waited until Moussa had fallen into a deep sleep, and then I went over to examine his private papers, which he never let out of his sight. I was taking precautions in view of the divorce.

I took what I needed, put it in an envelope, and then hid

it under my neighbour's doormat. I softly closed the door and locked it, and then I stole his bunch of keys, hid them under the carpet and went back to bed.

When he woke up, he took Ryad in his arms. 'My baby, my baby.'

'Oh, right, so now he's your baby!'

It had started. He began insulting my family, the first stage of a standard brawl in our community: your father, your mother, your brothers, etc.

I replied on the same subject with incredible vulgarity. I threw myself into it body and soul, feeling as if I were eating honey, until he retreated, saying, 'I'm out of here.'

'Oh, so you think you can just walk away like that? In your dreams!'

He dug around in his pockets looking for his keys, repeating, 'I'm out of here, I'm out of here.'

'You can look, but you won't find them! I've a score to settle with you; you don't decide when you leave. We have things to say to each other and we're going to say them! Your mother and you have driven me mad and you think you can just clear off like that?'

'Leila, let me open the door or this is going to end in tears.'

The atmosphere was becoming increasingly strained.

'Open that door or I'll jump out of the window!'

'That would suit me fine; I wouldn't be regarded as a divorcée, I'd be a widow! But you'll upset your beloved Maman!'

'Bloody hell, I don't know what's stopping me, I don't know what's stopping me!'

He punched the wall violently. I jumped with fright; if he'd punched me like that, he'd have floored me and I wouldn't be getting up anytime soon. However, I'd decided to push him to the limits at my own risk to ensure that we broke up. His insincerity was incredible.

'Have you any idea how much I've spent on you? Have you any idea how much you've cost me? My mother was nice – she brought a gift for Ryad and she gave you 100 francs!'

'Which came out of my account. You told me that yourself when you took it back!'

'Wasn't everything I spent on the wedding enough for you?'

Until then I had been holding back watching him struggle; I was in a position of strength. But now he had really annoyed me.

'Oh, is that it?'

I headed for the kitchen in the direction of the knife drawer and he began to panic.

'What are you doing?'

'Mind your own business; the best thing you can do is stay away from me. You'd better not come anywhere near me!'

I had picked up the large type of knife used to slit the throat of a sheep. I went into the bedroom, took out that bloody suitcase packed with wedding things, that wretched wedding dress, and shredded everything in front of him. Into tiny pieces. He saw his money and his wedding strewn across the room. I murdered my wedding dress first, a symbolic necessity since the first time I had tried to do it.

'She's completely crazy, the girl's completely crazy.'

'If it's your money you want, here, take it!'

All the dresses, djellabas, pairs of trousers, everything he had bought me, ended up in shreds, including the set of sheets we'd been given by his mother; I knew attacking them would be the last straw for him. He screamed, but he couldn't get near me because of that massive knife. I mimicked his mother, saying, 'And I brought a set of sheets, my son. I brought a set of embroidered sheets for my grandson! It's a horrible set of sheets.'

'Leila, don't do that, Leila, don't, they're Ryad's, they're a gift from his grandmother.'

'You can all go to hell. I don't want anything from any of you.'

'Leila, give them to me. I'll send them back to my mother so that she can reuse them.'

I cut them into pieces. 'Here, send them back to your mother now.'

He'd never seen me in such a state before and I'd never been as bad as that. God knows I was aggressive, but that day I was really violent and felt capable of worse. It was my turn to have some fun and no one else's. I think this marriage had really driven me crazy.

'Let me go out, just to get a breath of fresh air . . . '

'No, I'm keeping you locked up like I've been locked up. You're staying here.'

I was waiting for him to explode. I was pushing him as far as I could to make him hit me. It was the only way of obtaining something to use as a pretext for divorce. But he was going round and round in circles, begging me to give him the keys. This performance lasted the whole day. It was no good; the coward didn't lay a finger on me. So I temporarily gave up the fight, exhausted.

'If you want to get out now, then go. Here are the keys; open the door, but put them back on the table before you leave! I never want to see you again!'

He left, but as I'd suspected he would, he kept the keys, so he was coming back.

When I described the scene to my parents, my mother was pleased. She said, 'Come home, if you like.'

Definitely not.

My father said, 'What you've done is wrong. Remember you have a child with that man. If you go too far, he'll repudiate you.'

It's very difficult to remarry a repudiated daughter with a child. Her father no longer has any control over her and she can't live openly on her own. It's a vicious circle. I was paying the rent, but I didn't even have the right to show him the door: the lease was in the name of Mr and Mrs.

The two enemies watched each other. I went to work; my mother was looking after Ryad again as I didn't want to leave him alone with his father. Anyway, I would no longer let my son out of my sight. Moussa didn't work; his training scheme was finished so he stayed at home, sleeping, reading the Koran and hanging around in cafés. He didn't put anything away, not even the washing-up. During the week I'd come home from work as late as possible. I'd pop in to have a chat with my neighbours. I dawdled as much as possible before coming home to him, so that he'd finally decide that I was a bad wife and we would get a divorce. He held his ground. He was now sleeping in the lounge, while I slept in my bedroom. I couldn't bear him to touch me any more. I'd go to bed first; I'd fall asleep, and as soon as he tried to make a move, I'd say, 'I'm asleep.'

Finally he decided to hit me.

He started by being rough and vindictive. Every time he called his mother in Morocco, he'd be in a foul mood. He'd insult me. I'd reply and he'd hit me.

I wanted to lodge a complaint and my parents agreed in principle, but kept postponing the date. 'No, wait, give him one last chance. Think of your son.'

I would hit back, but I only weighed 7 stone and he was over 13 stone; he was tall, he'd catch hold of me easily and smash my head against the wall.

Then came the last time; the one that convinced me to lodge a complaint and go through with it.

One evening, at midnight, I was quietly taking a bath to relax and I'd forgotten to lock the bathroom door. He began to start a fight, me in the bath, him on the other side of the door, being spiteful. 'Your mother this, your mother that . . . your mother . . . '

Finally my family were all tarts, so my mother and I were tarts.

'All tarts! Both as bad as each other; you smoke cigarettes!'

I had an answer for every insult, in the firm belief that I was safe behind the door.

'Bloody tart!'

'Fine, so I'm a tart. As long as I'm not "your" tart, I don't care.'

In the end I'd had enough of this business with tarts, especially when talking about my mother. That's all men can say. You cut your hair; you're a tart, you smoke, you're a tart; you'd think they'd never seen a real tart in their life. I thought carefully and prepared what I was going to say first before I calmly came out with it.

'Your mother didn't stay with her first husband for more than a fortnight before he repudiated her, OK? After that she was dumped by force on your father to avoid disgracing the family. My mother has been married once in her whole life.'

He didn't know this family secret, which his mother's eldest sister had told me in confidence. To save family honour they had commandeered a cousin staying in the house and forced him to agree, because he was receiving board and lodging. However, the children didn't know about this, and it was particularly important that news of this disgrace shouldn't reach the ears of her daughters-in-law.

He dashed over to the phone to call his mother. I had just found a very effective argument, as I heard. The loudspeaker was on, as always, in his mother's house, and my sisters-in-law-heard everything. How had I, a stranger from the middle of France, gained access to this 'revelation'? My mother-in-law had a fit of hysterics. It was the worst possible insult, and I could be certain that she'd do everything in her power to make sure that I would also be repudiated in my turn – and it hadn't occurred to me soon enough.

Moussa was furious, his eyes popping out of his head. 'Bloody bitch, bloody tart, open this door!'

He was in the kitchen and the door was locked on that side; but the other door was open. I had time to reply, 'Yes, I know, we're all tarts as far back as my great-grandmother, but your mother is the biggest one of all.'

He walked round to the other door and charged into the bathroom. He shoved my head under the water. I struggled, managing to raise my head above the water, and scratched his face so badly that he bore the marks for ages. He seized me around the waist, threw me onto the floor, and then began to punch and kick my face and body; he battered me to a pulp in a matter of seconds.

'Is this what you want? Here, take that and that.'

Those punches and kicks raining down on my naked body were worse than anything. What I felt at that moment was indescribable. It was the total shame, humiliation and horror of a woman being stoned to death.

When he finally stopped I huddled under the washbasin. I

couldn't see clearly. Looking pleased with himself, he walked out of the bathroom.

After a while I bathed my face and went into the kitchen. I wanted to pick up a knife and plunge it anywhere in his body. I was in a complete state of crisis, but then I noticed something that stopped me dead in my tracks, just as if the electric power had been switched off: a photo of my son. I said to myself, 'If you do that, Leila, you're screwed; you'll have lost everything, you'll have lost your son, and he'll have won.'

He had noticed my movement and he saw the knife in my hand; I had picked it up without even realising it, so he was afraid.

'What are you doing? What are you doing?'

He locked himself in the toilet. I put on a djellaba and went out in the dark to ring at the door of one of my brothers, the one who lived nearest. He found me in tears on his doormat. When he saw the extent of my injuries he wanted to go and beat Moussa up. But brotherly revenge wasn't part of my plan.

'Drop it. No good will come of it if you get involved.'

This time my father told me to lodge a complaint at the police station. I needed a medical certificate. He had beaten me for such a long time, to the point of almost battering me to death, that virtually my whole body was black and blue. I was given a certificate at the hospital and at the police station. The policeman on duty said, 'Come now, it's just a quarrel! Think about it overnight before pressing charges. So many people begin proceedings, and then come back the next day hassling us to withdraw the charges! Take some time to think about it.'

I looked him straight in the eyes, and said, 'I want to press charges now and I'm not leaving until I do.'

I knew the hassle this would create. Everyone was going to come down on me like a ton of bricks. I was going to get it in the neck from my husband's parents and his family for daring to accuse him.

I signed the complaint and my brother took me home; he wanted me to stay at his place but I wanted to go home. I didn't want my enemy to think he'd won. Fortunately, my son never witnessed this sort of scene. So I went home at the risk of him starting on me again, but I knew what I was doing. I had warned the cops that I was going home.

He was smiling as he watched me come in and cross the room. 'Leila, come here, darling, and let me comfort you. It's a lot of fuss over nothing; it's just a quarrel. It's OK, we'll get over it.'

He would have been perfectly happy to take me to bed. I replied, 'Where do you think you're sleeping?'

'In our bed.'

I went into the kitchen and fetched the knife, holding it firmly, threateningly. 'You come near my room and I'll stab you!'

He looked at me incredulously.

'I repeat! You come near this room or this bed and I'll stab you.'

I went to bed, putting the knife on the bedside table. He hadn't said a word. He stayed in the lounge, but I didn't sleep that night; thoughts were buzzing round my head.

'Leila, this guy is your son's father, even if he's not interested in him, but if you don't press charges, you're screwed. You're 24, and if you aren't capable of separating from this man now, you'll never have the right to complain again. You have two alternatives. Either you do it now, while you still have a life in front of you, or you give up all hope and you wake up at the age of 40 having screwed up your life – and probably Ryad's too. Is that what you want? Your life behind you? Or will you wake up now with your life still in front of you?'

The next day my father stepped into the breach and I was summoned home.

'Leila, we've given it some thought. You must write a letter to the public prosecutor and drop the charges.'

'Papa, have you seen the state I'm in? Do you want to see the rest?'

'I told you to drop the charges. You have a child with that man!'

The fly was still trapped in its glass prison. I wrote the letter, but added at the end: 'Make no mistake, Monsieur le Procureur, I'm not doing this for me, but for my son, to give him the chance to grow up with his father in his life.'

It may have been that sentence that caused the public prosecutor to reject my request. I was summoned to the police station. I could no longer stop the proceedings. The summons was due to arrive at the conjugal home in ten days.

After that period of courage and aggressive behaviour, I became terribly depressed again and hit rock bottom. I was scaring everyone, because I was so skeletal. During those ten days, Moussa didn't touch me. He knew it wasn't worth him starting with me again and my brother had warned him. He'd told him, 'Listen, the trouble between you and my sister is your problem, but say one word about my father, my mother or one of us . . . and I'll slit your throat and drink your blood, I'll take your head to the police station and send your body to your mother!'

He had been so afraid that he'd gone to the police station to complain about death threats. I was ashamed about that

. . . About all these fights, blows and insults, ashamed at not being able just to ask for a divorce through a lawyer without any fuss.

After ten days the summons arrived and Moussa could read the charge against him for aggravated domestic assault. We both had to attend the hearing. He went there on his own and so did I. Moussa, looking uncommunicative, sat on the right before the public prosecutor's representative, while I sat stiffly on the left, feeling tense.

'Monsieur, have you ever beaten your wife?'

'No, absolutely not. But, you know, Monsieur le Procureur, I'm a Muslim and, make no mistake, a Muslim is permitted to beat his wife; that's the Islamic religion.'

The magistrate looked at him askance. 'Don't confuse matters. You are a Muslim, that's a fact. But this is a free country and here we don't use religion as a pretext to hit a woman.'

'It's not true, I didn't hit her, she's lying, you can't believe a word she says. Her brothers are always threatening me.'

'What about you, Madame? What do you have to say?'

I confirmed that he had beaten me. He had the certificate in front of him and you could still see where I had been hit, but Moussa interrupted me every couple of seconds. He wanted to stop me from explaining, and again brought up the matter of his religion that allowed a man to punish a bad wife if she deserved it.

This time the magistrate lost his temper and banged on the table. 'Monsieur! For the second time! Religion has nothing to do with this! Let Madame speak! Otherwise, you'll be shown out! It's in your interest to be sensible about this; it would be better for you to be present to hear what she has to say, instead of leaving her to talk in your absence!'

'She sleeps with a knife!'

It was true, but the magistrate didn't believe him; he had just interrupted me for the third time.

'Outside, Monsieur! Be quick about it!'

Hypocritically, he went to sit down near the door so that he could still hear.

'No, not there! In the room at the back! Officer, keep an eye on that man!'

He wasn't being so smart now; I suppose he had been humiliated in his own personal view of a husband's rights. The French residence permit he had obtained only recently had apparently not given him enough time to understand the idea of a republican state. In his view, men were always right and men and women weren't equal in the eyes of the law.

I accurately related the facts and the magistrate contemplated me for a while.

'What should we do? I'd be tempted to send him before a judge.'

'Perhaps that would be going too far. I'd just like him to know that there are laws in France and that he must obey them.'

The magistrate called Moussa back. Then he looked at me, and only me, insistently. 'So, you're happy? We agree? That's what we'll do?'

Moussa couldn't stand him saying that. It hit him right between the eyes. I'd been able to talk, someone had listened to me and, in some respects, I was the one deciding his sentence.

'I'm sentencing you to a one-year observation period for aggravated domestic assault. Look at me, Monsieur! I'm warning you: if anything happens to Madame, if you're unlucky enough to disturb a hair on her head, you will have me to reckon with!'

He had driven there in the car, while I'd come on foot. I'd been stupid enough to give the car back to him. I couldn't resist calling out to him, 'Hey, Moussa, it's OK; you can give me a lift home! We're going to the same place.'

'Sod off.'

'Fine! You married me for your papers, didn't you? You got them, didn't you? So why don't you get lost and leave me in peace.'

I thought he would run back to his mother or decide to live somewhere else. Four months went by and the atmosphere was very strained – he had a job, but was working part-time and his hours didn't coincide with mine, so I wasn't sure exactly what he was doing, but I was left more or less in peace. We just saw each other in passing most of the time.

I had filled out an application for maintenance at the court and he didn't know. Another registered letter arrived from the magistrate's court ordering him to declare his income so that they could work out what contribution he had to make towards household expenses. He started to cry! Pay to live in France? Pay for his son? He hadn't considered things from that angle.

One evening I was almost a goner. I can't remember how it started, but as I was still pushing him to the limit over the slightest thing, desperate for him to leave at last, he pinned me against the wall with his fist raised. I confidently looked him straight in the eye. 'Moussa, a year's suspended sentence! Remember? That's all I've been waiting for, so go ahead.'

He let me go, but he was infuriated by the fact that he couldn't hit me, as he'd wanted. He began to strike himself, screaming, 'I'm sick to death of this girl, I'm sick to death of this girl! I want to make a success of my life. I don't want my son to grow up all alone and my mother isn't here!'

He punched himself so badly that his face and eyes were swollen; it was unbearable to watch. He was acting so crazily that I panicked and told him to calm down. He wasn't listening; he was banging his head against the walls, rolling around on the floor, and then beginning all over again, I couldn't bring him under control. I had to call the neighbours for help, and then an ambulance. One of my neighbours worked in a hospital and she had never seen an attack like this.

I'd already seen him put on an act, like his mother, but it was impossible for him to be play-acting to this extent. He was completely delirious. His face was swollen and blood-stained and he was hurling himself against the wall, clawing his chest and tearing his clothes. If he had grabbed hold of me when he was like that, he would have killed me, and I was really afraid of him this time. The man was mentally ill.

The emergency services refused to come when they found out that he was suffering from a fit of madness. We had to call the police and a doctor. They gave him two injections of Valium to calm him down, and then he was carted off to hospital. As usual, I had a tetany attack. I felt guilty; I'd gone too far. It was all very well for the doctor to say that he could've killed me while having a fit like that, that it wasn't 'normal' to react in that way during a domestic scene, I still felt it was my fault. It was always my fault. I should have let him insult me and kept quiet. But how do people stay silent for ever? Kicked from pillar to post as a teenager, a forced marriage, a hysterical mother-in-law, a hysterical husband, I was becoming hysterical myself.

After an injection, on my own at home, I was still turning it over in my head. 'When it comes down to it, you're not guilty of anything; you're just defending yourself with the weapons at your disposal. What other choice do you have? Use the knife to kill him? I'm not a criminal. Or run off with my kid, but where to? If I go to my father's house, he tells me: "Drop the charges, don't get divorced!" So where else? Should I end up in a hostel for battered wives somewhere? With a bed, my kid and a suitcase. And what about my job? And my flat? Let my husband live there in peace and quiet, while my baby and I live in one room and exist on income support? It's either that or return to my parents. Go back there after everything I've done to escape from the trap? So that I can hear it said non-stop: "He's going to repudiate you! He's repudiated you, we told you that would happen! Where are you going? Who with? What time will you be back? Have you been smoking?"'

I felt as if I were choking; I had to get out of the flat, I had to talk to someone. In the middle of the night and in my situation, Maryvonne was the only person who came to mind. When she looked at me, it was as if she were looking in a mirror. Same story except for the fact that she hadn't hesitated to use a knife and slash her husband when he had wanted to throw their baby out of the window. She had run away and he'd never seen his wife or child again. One keepsake: a scar for life.

Maryvonne let me cry and waited. 'Have you had an attack?'

'No, I haven't slept.'

'Come off it! You're black and blue!'

'It's nothing. It's my husband; he's driving me crazy. I get panic attacks. Do you have something to help me sleep? I can't sleep at all.'

I had already been walking around in circles for an hour

in the neighbourhood. Maryvonne had to give me what I needed. I didn't want to worry her. However, I really looked lousy. In the end, I told her a little about Moussa's attack and the fright I'd had.

'You ought to go to the doctor, Leila. You're far too depressed.'

'I'm going back tomorrow. He gave me some tranquillisers, but I've run out.'

She gave me half a box of tranquillisers, advising me to take a quarter of a tablet at a time if I had a panic attack.

I said I was feeling better and went home with the little box. There was still blood on the floor, smears of blood on the wall and on the sofa. I called my sister-in-law in Morocco to tell her what had happened. 'I think I've driven him mad. I think it's my fault! Why did I do that?'

'Listen, Leila, both mother and son are notorious for putting on an act. They're mad! Don't let it get to you. He's in hospital, they're looking after him and he'll get better.'

I pretended to be convinced and hung up the receiver, but I kept thinking, 'Why did I do that. I've driven him mad.'

I swallowed the contents of a box of tranquillisers that I already had in my medicine cabinet along with what Maryvonne had given me. Before that I had performed my evening ablutions and placed the Koran under my pillow. I wanted to go to sleep or die in peace; I didn't really know. At any rate, I wanted to stop thinking. The next day my mother thought I was sleeping peacefully, so she didn't wake me right away. She'd come to tidy the house after that hellish night. Then she shook me. I opened my eyes after a fashion; I could barely stand, but I took a shower, dressed and staggered to my office. I sat down, but when I tried to get up, I collapsed in a heap. To cap it all I wasn't even supposed to be working that morning, but I'd forgotten.

I woke up in hospital with someone leaning over me, asking, 'Is she an alcoholic? A drug addict?'

I opened my eyes, looking around wildly, terrified at the idea that they might have me locked away.

CHAPTER TEN

How do you talk about love?

I WANTED TO GET out of that room as quickly as possible. They'd sent a shrink to see me, but I hadn't opened my mouth. I had botched another suicide attempt and it was sickening. Was I simply going mad? Did I really want to die? Malika, a friend from the neighbourhood, had rushed to my bedside. Both she and my parents thought I had suffered an attack of tetany. Another one. So I kept quiet and stubbornly refused to eat in the foolish hope that the doctor would become discouraged and let me go home. Moussa had been taken to the psychiatric ward and I certainly didn't want to end up in there with him.

My youngest brother rushed in, panic-stricken. 'Leila! Get up! Moussa has been discharged from hospital. He telephoned home to say that he's coming to get Ryad.'

Panic. He was going to take my son away from me, take him back to Morocco to his mother's house. I clambered out of bed. I wanted to dress, but they had taken my clothes and I was on a drip. I screamed, 'Let me go!'

The nurse ran in, followed by the doctor. 'I can't let you leave here like that. You're too ill. You haven't talked to the psychologist; he has to come back and see you.'

'You have to let me go! If I have to hit you, I will, but I'm going.'

Malika tried to calm me down. 'Don't worry, I'll go to your place and find out what's going on.'

She dashed out, but nothing could calm me down; this was about Ryad, my life.

No one understood, since no one there knew my story. Married by force? Me, never. Suicidal? Never. But my son, my little man, my only source of happiness in this lousy life, I couldn't leave him in the hands of that violent madman. He was mine.

I ripped out the drip and pushed the doctor away, screaming, 'Leave me alone! My son, he's going to take my son away, he's going to take my son away from me.'

I fell to my knees and beat on the floor with my fists. 'He's going to take my son away from me; if he takes my son, I've got nothing left to live for, nothing left to make life worth living, I must get my son back.'

I looked at them through my tears. I begged the doctor and the nurses, I clutched at their white coats. 'I want my son, I'm begging you!'

'You're not in a fit state to sign a discharge.'

'I'll sign whatever you want, but I must get my son back! Do you understand? I have to get my son back, before he takes him away from me!'

Finally, he agreed to let me sign a discharge, but only after a good half-hour, and I rushed out like a lunatic in my pyjamas and slippers, without bothering to wait for my clothes. I was still running along the road, panting, my legs like cotton wool, when a car pulled up alongside me and I heard someone shout, 'Leila, stop.'

'No, no! My son, I have to get my son back!'

Malika got out of the car and ran after me. 'Stop! Ryad is in my car. Your mother is with me.'

I kept trembling with fear. I wasn't listening to anything she said to me. 'Malika, he's going to take my son!'

While I was arguing the toss in the hospital, Malika had gone to fetch my mother and Ryad. She had to slap me to bring to me to my senses and make me realise that Ryad was there, in my mother's arms. I hugged him hard enough to smother him.

I should have gone back to the hospital. I realise now how ill I was. However, at that time, I couldn't put a name to my illness. I refused to lower my guard. Admitting to depression was tantamount to denying myself. It was part of me; I had been living with it for years as if it were a double of myself. Fear is a real illness. I'd been made to feel afraid of everything: of being a girl, of my virginity, my rebellions, marriage, and now I was afraid for my son. In a nutshell, I was afraid of living. I couldn't admit it as easily then as I can now because I was still afraid; I was surrounded by fear. At times it was so suffocating that I tried to die or to call for help. Whether I had a fit of hysterics or the giggles, it amounted to the same thing. The fly was flapping around clumsily, as best it could.

I refused to leave my home and go back to live with my parents. The limited freedom I had won for myself was too precious. I wouldn't have any freedom any more with my family. I didn't want any medical or psychological help either, convinced that I had to stand on my own two feet. But I was anorexic, weak and desperately alone in that crazy existence, caught between the fear of living and the fear of dying.

So I went home with my son, all seven stone of me. I wouldn't take my eyes off Ryad. He went everywhere with me. From the bedroom to the kitchen and even to the toilet, I wouldn't let him out of my sight again. Ryad was just over a year old then. I fastened him around my neck like a necklace; you would have had to kill me to take him away from me.

Ryad's father had managed to leave hospital after 48 hours, explaining that his attack had merely been the result of 'trouble with his wife', who wanted a divorce. He presented himself in the best possible light. For almost a year I dragged myself from sick leave to sick leave watched by a man who'd become violent because he couldn't dominate me.

We didn't talk any more. We were two strangers living under the same roof. I continued to play my role as a housewife, doing his washing, preparing the evening meal – the bare minimum. I didn't go out with him, not even to run an errand. I never left him alone with Ryad because I was so afraid that he'd take him back to his mother. He earned a living, but he sent most of his wages back to his mother. In the autumn of that year, he went back to Morocco, knowing full well that he had been summoned to appear before a judge to sort out the maintenance he was supposed to pay. He thought I was going withdraw my application for fear of being repudiated.

So I went to the hearing alone; he had sent a medical certificate to his lawyer, whom he wasn't even paying since he'd applied for legal aid. The father of my son was allegedly suffering from depression and couldn't attend the hearing. Case postponed until the following month.

I dissolved in tears in front of the judge. I was sick to death of this continual play-acting. Paying for nothing, taking everything. That was the objective. Take a wife to acquire French citizenship and then exploit the situation to the maximum. The same thing happened at the second hearing. The judge wanted to postpone the case again, but this time Moussa's own lawyer declared that he couldn't ethically continue to defend the man. 'I know him. He'll never turn up. He'll always find a way over there to ask to be excused for reasons of illness. There will be no end to it and his wife is the one who suffers.'

The judge agreed and Moussa was sentenced to pay an allowance to his wife and son. Two hundred euros a month. This wasn't a huge sum, but that 'family man' regarded this decision as an insult to his wallet. He had a family member telephone me to make me change my mind. He wrote to the judge appealing against the decision that had been taken in his absence. And he came back to France at top speed, but he didn't come home. He buried himself somewhere in the provinces, claiming he had no money and living in a rehabilitation centre. I only heard from him officially.

I was summoned to the Moroccan consulate on the grounds of repudiation. I went in the knowledge that the procedure could only take place before the Aduls and not in France. There was a fresh summons to appear before the Judge of Family Affairs in Morocco, in which Moussa accused me of adultery, obviously without any proof and still without attending. The hearing was postponed. Personally, I was determined to obtain a divorce in France.

As the repudiation still hadn't been recorded, my parents continued to cling to this sham marriage and family honour. 'He'll come back, you must phone him and ask him for forgiveness.'

Forgiveness? Forgiveness for marrying him by force? Never!

They had wanted this marriage; my father had beaten me for it and despite its failure and all the suffering I'd experienced, they still seemed to feel that repudiation was the worse thing that could happen to me. And they were using it to regain control, not only over my life and choices, but also over my social behaviour.

One evening I'd gone to a restaurant with some work colleagues. I'd come home at 9.30 p.m. My brother phoned me, and said, 'You're in for it! Papa knows you went out! He wants to see you!'

I told myself that I had to cut the umbilical cord now or never. My father was waiting for me in the torture room, his hands behind his back. 'Where were you?'

My mother started to insult me. 'Only tarts go out at this late hour!'

My father told her to be quiet. It was up to him to deal with the 'problem'. 'Come here! Where were you?'

'I was at a restaurant with some colleagues.'

'Do you think this is an appropriate time to go out?'

'Papa, it's 9.30 in the evening; it's no big deal! I can go to a restaurant without . . . '

'No! You've no business going out if you're going to come back as late as this. Come here! Breathe in my face.'

It was starting all over again. A woman who goes out and smokes is a tart, never mind if she's 24 years old or married.

'You've been smoking!'

He spat in my face and insulted me in Arabic. 'Get out! You're no better than a tart! Moussa was right about everything; you're just a bad wife!'

My mother added, 'I'm not surprised he left! Why should

a man stay with you! Even if you marry 15 times, you'll get divorced 15 times. You smoke cigarettes; you're nothing but a slut!'

And my father finished me off, by spitting at me again, 'You disgust me!'

I was paralysed. What had I prepared myself to say to them? I didn't remember. Or rather, I did, I wanted to tell them, 'Bloody hell, leave me alone, haven't I given you enough? Let me live my life! I haven't done anything wrong. I went to a restaurant; I haven't shown my backside to the whole world!'

However, I had a mental block: I couldn't do it. I stood there, keyed up, my fists clenched at the terrible unfairness of it. 'It's your fault, you're the guilty one.' I could hear anything, I could take anything, except 'Moussa is right. You're a bad wife.'

My father concluded, 'From now on you either get back on the straight and narrow, or you can cope on your own with your son; you don't have a family any more! I never want to see you again.'

I can still see myself face to face with him in that room when he said to me, 'You'll marry him! It's him and no other, otherwise you're no longer part of this family!'

He was breaking my heart. I'll never be free because of that and I'm not the only one. They know they have a hold over us. The family keeps us safe in a world we haven't learned to master on our own. This is because that world is denied to us from childhood and because we end up there without any resources, without a personal structure, conditioned by traditions, taboos and fear. It is also because we love our parents. A North African girl is almost incapable of cutting the umbilical cord. She might want to; she's always looking for a pair of scissors to do the deed and then, at the last moment, the fear of being abandoned, repudiated and alone in the world prevents her from finding them. This umbilical cord is strangling us, choking us to death, even when we've been born in France. I had left home twice and I had come back. Fear of freedom, fear of flying because my wings had been clipped. I no longer knew who I was. Leila, a father's daughter, Leila, a stranger's wife, or Leila, a little boy's mother. The latter was the only thing I was certain of but, even on that level, my parents were blackmailing me with him to keep control. 'If you don't get back on the straight and narrow . . . ' It was the straight and narrow path of submission and everything that went with it, everything that had made me ill.

I'd tried to top myself because they'd taken my life away from me; they didn't care. I was the one who wasn't normal.

I wanted to die again. I really did want to. To have done with it all for good. I was sick to death, at the end of my tether – even my son was no longer enough to bind me to this shitty life, where I was always guilty, always punished, always locked away.

I took hold of the Koran, as if asking God to come with me. I swallowed all the antidepressants I'd been given at the hospital and started to read verses at random in the quiet flat. And then I went under again.

'Leila, can you hear me? Leila, can you hear me!'

I could hear. It was vague, indistinct. I'd been put on a drip where I was. I'd botched another suicide attempt. When my mother tried to take me in her arms, I pulled back rebelliously and screamed, 'Leave me alone, just go away, I don't want you in my life any more.'

'I'm your mother, your mother . . . '

'Leave me alone, you're not my mother, leave me alone.'

I was screaming and crying at the same time.

'Leila, what's wrong? This is your Papa speaking.'

'Leave me alone, leave me alone . . . '

I just kept repeating that phrase: 'Leave me alone.'

I didn't realise he was unhappy and concerned, that he genuinely wanted me to be happy and that he found my attitude completely incomprehensible. There was nothing surprising about the effect this had. My father condemned me again. 'You've humiliated us in front of everyone!'

That night, I'd sent a message of farewell to Martine, the street worker who'd been monitoring my progress closely and to whom I owe my life. She protected me, talked to me and, without knowing my story inside out, was desperate for me to undergo treatment.

'Go and see a psychiatrist, Leila.'

'No way.'

I'd thought she wouldn't receive the message before morning and that by then I'd be dead. I had miscalculated.

All my brothers were sitting at home in the lounge. My friend was the only white French woman there. It was hard for them to have a conversation, but she was the only one who could have broached the subject.

'She doesn't have the right to do that. We don't get divorced in our community; she must wait for him to come back. She has a child, and she doesn't have the right to any other type of life.'

'Why shouldn't she be allowed another type of life? Don't you think she's paid a high enough price? Are you waiting for your sister to die? You should be on her side, helping her to cope.'

I was taken to the hospital to have my stomach pumped. Then they wanted to make me eat, but I knocked the tray flying. They sent me a shrink, but I sent the shrink packing. With the blanket over my head, I refused to see anyone or listen to anyone and, above all, I didn't want to be asked any questions. I didn't even know what the questions were any more. The psychiatrist stood by my bed for a moment in silence, and then he went to tell the doctor, 'Transfer her to the psychiatric hospital!'

The doctor came to my room. He sent out the nurse and closed the door behind her. 'Now, Leila, you're going to get up! Come on! Get up!'

He made me get out of bed and began speaking to me as if we were close friends, looking me straight in the eye. 'I'm a Muslim and I'm a doctor, so I'll explain things to you so that you understand properly. So you want to die?'

'Yes.'

'You have a son, don't you? You love him, don't you?'

'Yes.'

'Do you want to lose him? If you do, this is the best way to go about it, so try again! Now pay close attention: you have two options. Either you decide to get better and move, or you'll be transferred to the psychiatric hospital tomorrow morning. And, this time, you'll lose your son for a very long time. But if you promise to make an effort to get better, I'll call your father immediately. As we are both Muslims, he'll have to listen to me! What is it that's bothering him? He doesn't wants you to get divorced?'

'It's a sin. It's "halam"!'

'I shall tell him that divorce is "halal"! It's permitted by our religion when a couple no longer sees eye to eye. Even in Morocco, the king has decided to allow divorce! So what's your decision? I'm fed up of seeing you brought in here half dead with your calls for help! One fine day you won't make a mess of it and you'll succeed. I have absolutely no desire to visit you in the mortuary. Well? It's up to you – have you decided?'

'Yes, OK.'

'OK? You promise?'

'Yes, I promise.'

He called my father there and then to ask him for a meeting, determined not to let him wriggle out of it by claiming he had some commitment or other. This doctor had in fact figured out about the forced marriage and the parental pressure, and he'd seen me in a bad way too often on his ward.

'Let me make myself clear, Monsieur. I want to see you tomorrow morning at 8 o'clock; if you aren't here then, you'll lose your daughter for good; it's off to the psychiatric hospital with her! The transfer is due to take place at 10.30 in the morning! Thank you, goodnight.'

I doubt if anyone had ever talked to my father in that tone of voice. If it had been a French doctor, it wouldn't have worked.

The next day my father was on time. They talked for nearly an hour in private. Finally, a man was standing up for me – not just with the authority of his profession but, most importantly, with that of his religious beliefs.

'It's done: I've talked to your father. I told him that things were no longer working out with your husband; that divorce was perfectly "halal" and that he had to accept it. You must also accept it; a woman isn't guilty for wanting a divorce. Now, get dressed. I don't want to see you in here again for anything more than a sprained ankle!'

My father was waiting for me at the exit. He didn't say a word to me, didn't look at me. My mother was at home with my son. I went straight to my bedroom like a zombie, closed the shutters and went to bed. She ventured into the room to wake me up and get me to eat something.

'Get out.'

I hadn't even seen it was her. I was saying 'Get out' to the whole world.

I was at my lowest ebb. For almost three weeks I hadn't eaten or drunk anything and I had started to dehydrate. The doctor had only prescribed vitamins for me in case I tried to overdose again. I was letting myself waste away, like a camel abandoned in the desert. I couldn't get out of bed or move at all. I'd put myself to bed to die.

Ryad tried to enter the room from time to time, but I didn't realise. My mother was always there, crying, powerless to feed me, and I didn't care. So, she called my friend Maryvonne to come to the rescue. 'I don't know what to do any more. No one is allowed to go into her room, she lies there in the dark, she won't eat, she won't drink, my daughter is going to die. I sense that my daughter's going to die.'

Maryvonne, the good-natured 'mamma', charged into my room in a rage. 'What nonsense is this?'

'Get out, Maryvonne, get out; I don't want to see you.'

'You think you're getting out of it like that? That's too easy!'

She opened the shutters. I put my head under the covers, screaming, 'Bloody hell, Maryvonne, you've no right coming into my home like this, get out.'

'Take my word for it; you're going to get up! I can assure you that you're going to get up. And I'm taking you to the doctor today! From the look of you, I've no desire to have your death on my conscience.'

She dragged me out of bed. Maryvonne is a 14-stone force

of nature and I was as light as a feather, being shaken unceremoniously.

'Look at your mother! Look at your mother crying! Look at your son! I went through this and even I didn't go to pieces like you. I didn't let myself die like you're doing! You have a son. He's asked for absolutely nothing. Shift your arse, we're leaving!'

The family doctor actually slapped me when he saw me in that state. He also threatened to send me to the psychiatric hospital. My friends intervened, because I was in danger of losing custody of my son. They tried to find a room for me in a convalescent home, but it was impossible. So I went back home, still acting like a zombie. My mother was taking care of Ryad on the other side of the door to my room, where I hid myself away.

I would only get up to look out of the window from time to time. The empty space. I was fascinated by that empty space. I'd get up, I'd gaze out of it and then I'd go back to bed. I thought to myself that the day would come when I'd be brave enough to do it. Tomorrow perhaps. It was like a daily ritual. What if I jumped?

I was laboriously taking the vitamins that the doctor had given me, but no one could make me eat and I still wasn't drinking. All I could manage was a little water on my lips. Swallowing had become almost impossible. When night fell I'd be filled with panic. I kept thinking about death; it was obsessive and awful to long for death without being brave enough to jump out of the window. One evening I tried to slit my wrists, but it wasn't enough, so I tried to strangle myself with a belt. However, the cordless phone was on my bed; it rang and instinctively I replied.

When it came down to it, I didn't want to die. I just wanted to show 'them' that I could die because of them. 'They' were my parents, particularly my father. For me to pull through, he would have had to acknowledge that he'd made a mistake and that he was to blame. But every time I tried to die, someone or something stopped me. Perhaps it was me – the other me, who was lying dormant within this suicidal anorexic body.

Someone said to me one day that I was so unhappy and so unable to think clearly that I was trying to say to my father, 'I want to exist for you by dying; I want to be proved right by dying.'

I was incapable of thinking about this then. I had been brainwashed. All I could think was, 'I want to die.' End of story.

Then, after 18 days of panic attacks and anorexia, that inner death decided by the brain, something happened. The door of the room opened a crack and a little mouse slipped in: Ryad, my son. He climbed onto my bed and clambered onto me; he straddled his mummy's chest and laid his head in the crook of my neck.

I heard his little voice saying, 'You know, Maman, I love you. I love you very much, I'll love you for ever.'

Miraculously, that little voice came at a time when other voices, those of the friends who loved me and others who thought they loved me, hadn't been getting through for ages.

I realised that I didn't have the right to do 'this' to my little man. He was my life and I was his. Without me, he would suffer. Without me, he'd fall victim to an upbringing that I was rejecting.

It was him and me 'for ever', as he said. Death went out of the window.

He had found the right button to press to get me back on my feet. I suddenly remembered everything clearly – the moment I'd learned I was pregnant, the glow of sheer happiness when I was talking to him as he lay cradled in my womb: 'I promise you that, whatever happens, I'll always be there for you, there are two of us now, for ever!'

If I went away and left him alone, I wouldn't be keeping my promise. I think he was the one who saved me. Ryad, my garden, my ray of light.

I took him in my arms and hugged him tightly. 'I'll love you too for ever; I'll always love you. Don't be afraid, Mummy will always be here.'

First, I sat up. Then I had to stand up. If I managed that, I would have won. I walked to the lounge tensing my muscles to stay upright and switched on the television. Ryad didn't leave my side for a second; he sat down beside me and together we looked at the images. In the evening I managed to swallow a small piece of bread and slowly drink a glass of water, while he ate his supper opposite me. It was hard to keep it up, but I resisted the urge to go back to bed. For him.

Gradually, I began to see life in colour again, although it looked strange at first, like an unfinished watercolour, never flamboyant, but in the end acceptable.

After months and months of paperwork, red tape, summonses to Morocco and France and resurgent feelings of hatred now and then, I obtained my separation, much to the humiliation of my father and mother. My father no longer expressed it violently, but it was always there.

Later, much later, I also tried to obtain my father's forgiveness, respect and, especially, his love. 'Between you and me, Papa, you know that I never wanted that husband!'

'It's past history, daughter, we can't turn the clock back.'

'But Papa, if you'd listened to me, it would never have come to this! He obtained French nationality, which was all he wanted. He proved that to you! He used you just like he used me. What did you gain from all this? Who gained anything in our family?'

And finally I heard the words I'd been waiting so long to hear. 'It was a mistake.'

I gained Ryad, but I still didn't have the freedom to live my life in broad daylight. A forced marriage is a family secret. In the complete confusion that brought me close to death, I remained convinced that God wanted nothing to do with a 'tradition' that tries to destroy the love between people. Girls married by force don't dare to admit to it. They lie to other people and invent storybook lives. I claimed to have met my husband on holiday. Others pretend that they've loved the stranger their father picked for them all their lives or they walk around constantly plagued by the 'shame' of being repudiated. Lying, pretending, keeping quiet, obeying and being submissive, reporting every little thing she does in her life to the men, the family and the neighbourhood: I couldn't bear the thought of a future like that.

I wasn't brave enough or happy-go-lucky enough, like other girls, to run away from my parents, whom I love but who were unintentionally suffocating me. I personally wanted to fight from within. To have enough guts to change their minds; to prove to my father, mother and brothers that we're entitled to have the freedom to live our lives and to love. I failed, because I was stubbornly determined to fight on my own.

I managed not to die because of Martine and my friends, who never let me go under. At the time, this was my only victory. I have won many others since then.

I've learned how to be independent without hurting others, just by endeavouring to understand them. I love my father. I've always loved him. I wouldn't want anyone to think otherwise and that my story is a means of settling scores with him. I know exactly when I should have been brave enough to say to him, 'Papa, I love you, but I don't want this stranger. Papa, I love you, but my answer is no.'

It should have been right at the start. Instead of walking into the lounge to meet my future husband with a tray of revolting tea, and instead of slyly provoking him, I should have accepted the help offered me by Martine and my friends to achieve my objective. I should have initiated a conversation and stood firm, instead of fighting like a militant rebel with all the violence I could muster, which brought me to the brink of suicide. There is always someone in the neighbourhood or the town capable of taking up your cause. If I have one piece of advice for other girls, it's to speak out. I implore them not to retreat into a proud, foolish silence, as I did.

Another victory: my parents have gradually become much more open-minded. They've adapted and evolved and have realised that the tradition of forced marriage trapped us and made us all suffer. My father never played with his own sons the way he plays with Ryad. They adore each other and he takes his grandson everywhere. Since his birth Ryad has made him very happy, and I am so happy to have given him to my father.

My relationship with my parents has changed. I was never able to see them before as I see them now. They've always loved each other and my father has always done his utmost to give us a good life. He's never raised a hand towards my mother, and I've never heard them tearing each other apart the way I did with Moussa. They were both heavily dependent on a tradition from another era and they believed it was relevant to their daughter. My hard, confused battle may have had the merit of making them realise that, and I know my little sister won't have to go through it: my experience has permanently protected her. Although I'm not a heroine, I believe I can say that, within my family at any rate, I'm a pioneer in this respect. I sometimes think back emotionally to the morning after my wedding in the lobby of that sumptuous hotel in Morocco and my impending wedding night. My father was crying when he took me in his arms. He loves me; he was sincere and didn't want to hurt me. I was not fighting against him, but against tradition, and I went about it in the wrong way. Anger and rage make it impossible to think clearly.

Another victory, and not the least important one, is that I now live on my own with my son, in *my* flat, although close enough to my family to make the most of them.

The last victory that remains to be won is Ryad's upbringing. One day I'll have to tell him about his father and make him understand that Moussa was bound as much as I was by an age-old system that continues to hold sway in certain families, and that he absolutely doesn't deserve to be hated for that. We were both victims.

Ryad, my son, I have paved the way for you; you won't be a male chauvinist or your mother's slave. One day you'll be free to love the woman of your choice and I'll make you the solemn promise that I'll never be a possessive, shrewish mother-in-law.

I have begun a long course of psychotherapy, which was essential for me and which I had refused for much too long. I'm beginning to know myself and, as a result, to know other people better; I hope with all my heart that I am and will stay a mother who deserves the love of her son.

I'm still afraid of the future; I'm particularly afraid of a husband's love because it's something I miss and dread in equal measure. I'm still, sometimes, an agitated fly, but I'm flying with my own wings, my son, and they'll carry us both. I'm now strong enough to do so. However, I can only present this story to the world anonymously. What I have described, as accurately and as honestly as possible, would be condemned by some who would consider it an intolerable challenge to their outmoded convictions. I must protect those I love from that. For the time being. One day, and I hope it is in my lifetime, my story will finally be ancient history.